An Insignificant Nobody

(Life Experiences)

by

John Ernest Day

Comedic anecdotes, prose/poetry,

biographical snippets, old sayings revisited,

quirky quips and quotes.

Something old, something new, something borrowed, with

something blue.

Humorous sayings with nonsensical phrases

bringing smiles to everyday faces.

Copyright © 2025 John Ernest Day

Dedication

I dedicate this publication to my beloved wife, Dawn, in celebration of thirty-four wonderful years of marriage.

Fifteen years ago, she endured a life-threatening trauma and underwent two exceptionally rare surgical procedures. Her life was saved by two remarkable surgeons, to whom she remains profoundly grateful.

About The Author

John Ernest Day grew up during the final years of World War II and the post-war era in Britain. His childhood was shaped by rationing, industrial pollution, and close-knit community life, with vivid memories of air raids and "Doodlebug" bombs near his home. Family life was complex and poignant: his father, a sea-going fisherman, died at sea at the age of thirty-six; his strict and superstitious mother influenced his early life; and his younger sister Barbara faced health challenges later in life.

Day's early education and childhood experiences — from trips to London during Queen Elizabeth II's coronation preparations to youthful adventures by the sea — fostered his love of poetry and storytelling. Despite struggling with asthma and school subjects, he cultivated a passion for writing that embraced a simple, accessible style, blending humour, reflection, and social commentary.

His literary pursuits include poetry, whimsical quips, and thoughtful reflections on love, loneliness, and society. He fondly recalls sending his work and artwork to notable figures such as Spike Milligan and Sir George Martin, highlighting his personal connection to the literary and artistic world.

Day also served in the Royal Air Force, training as a cook and serving in locations including Norfolk, Scotland, and Libya, where he experienced the challenges and camaraderie of military life. His post-military career spanned diverse roles such as security officer, toilet attendant, and car park inspector, all recounted with humour and candid observation.

A lifelong observer of social change, Day reflects on issues such as community preservation, urban planning, and immigration, sharing his personal opinions while celebrating humour, nostalgia, and nature. His love of the sea, countryside, and childhood memories infuses his work with warmth, creativity, and a hopeful spirit.

Acknowledgements

I would like to express my deepest gratitude to Janet Millar and the exceptional team at Writer Cosmos. Their dedication, expertise, and unwavering support have transformed the ambition of this publication into a reality. Without their guidance and encouragement, this work would not have reached its full potential.

Introduction

This extensive document is a rich tapestry of autobiographical reflections, humourous quips, poetry, and nostalgic anecdotes by John Ernest Day. It captures the essence of a life shaped by historical events, personal experiences, and a deep appreciation for the small, often overlooked moments that define human existence. The narrative spans childhood memories, family history, military service, creative pursuits, and social observations, all interwoven with wit and sentiment.

Early Life and Family Background

John Ernest Day reflects on his upbringing during the final years of World War II and post-war Britain, highlighting the hardships of rationing, pollution, and community life in industrial towns. He was born in Hitchin in 1943 but registered in 1944, with vivid memories of wartime incidents such as the "Doodlebug" bombs and air raids near his home.

His family life is detailed through portraits of his father, a sea-going fisherman who died at sea at age 36; his strict and superstitious mother; and his younger sister Barbara, who faced health challenges later in life. The narrative conveys the complexities of family relationships, including fear, love, and loss.

Childhood and Education

Day shares his school experiences, including his struggles with asthma, physical education, and academic subjects like arithmetic. He recounts moments of joy, such as a trip to London for Queen Elizabeth II's coronation decorations and early exposure to poetry that later inspired his writing.

He also describes his first job as a shop assistant and various youthful adventures near the sea, emphasising the innocence and freedom of childhood in a close-knit community.

Creative Pursuits and Literary Work

The author discusses his passion for writing poetry and prose, inspired by wartime poets and literary figures. He acknowledges his lack of formal literary training but embraces a simple, accessible style. His works range from humorous quips and nonsensical phrases to serious reflections on loneliness, love, and societal issues.

He also shares anecdotes about sending his artwork and writing to famous personalities like Spike Milligan and Sir George Martin, highlighting the personal significance of these connections.

Military Service and Work Experience

Day recounts his time in the Royal Air Force, training as a cook and serving in various locations, including Norfolk, Scotland, and Libya. He vividly describes the demanding nature of bulk catering, the camaraderie among servicemen, and humorous incidents from military life.

His post-military career includes diverse roles such as security officer, toilet attendant, and car park inspector, each depicted with candid observations and humour about the challenges and absurdities encountered.

Reflections on Society and Personal Opinions

Throughout the document, Day offers commentary on social changes, immigration, and contemporary issues, expressing concerns based on his experiences and observations. These controversial views are presented as personal opinions from the document without endorsement.

He also reminisces about the loss of historic buildings and community spirit, advocating for preservation and thoughtful urban planning.

Humour and Quirky Sayings

Interspersed are numerous quirky quips, jokes, and playful poems that provide levity and showcase Day's wit. These range from light-hearted wordplays to satirical takes on everyday life, reflecting a lifelong engagement with humour as a coping and creative tool.

Nature, Nostalgia, and Final Thoughts

The author expresses a deep connection to nature, particularly the sea and countryside, and shares nostalgic reflections on childhood games, local landmarks, and the passage of time. He acknowledges the challenges of ageing and health but maintains a hopeful and creative spirit.

The document closes with a heartfelt wish for peace and happiness, encapsulating a life lived with resilience, creativity, and a desire to connect with others through words and memories.

Early Life and Family Background

Nostalgic? Of course. As an octogenarian, I consider my own experiences from babyhood might be of interest in relating incidents during eras when existence differed immensely from that of today. World War II was in its final years, and food rationing created a frugal existence for millions throughout Great Britain. Smog (smoke-laden, thick fog) from industrial cities claimed many lives due to polluted air, and lung disorders were commonplace. Gas lamps illuminated streets. Bottles of milk were delivered daily to homes. Bread, cakes, rolls, and butcher's orders were collected from trade bikes. Paraffin for heating arrived on a donkey cart, poured from spouted, polished metal containers. Coal was brought to homes fortnightly and tipped into wooden bunkers next to outside toilets. A rent man collected dues from each household. Visiting gypsy folk (grandfather called them tinks) sold lucky Irish white heather, wooden clothes pegs for washing lines, or posies of flowers. Another man repaired frying pans and enamel washing-up bowls. People paid as much as they could afford into a Coop or Prudential Life Assurance Company for a rainy day.

Recycling enabled everyone to save newspapers (if they bought one) to earn a few extra pence. A bobby (police officer) did his rounds for security and stopped for a chat. And a cuppa. It was all quite acceptable.

Occasionally, the "nit nurse" paid a visit with her special comb to eliminate tiny unwanted nits from kids' hair. Lots of families had it. It was not painful.

I was not born in Lowestoft, a once-thriving herring-fishing industry town, but in Hitchin, Hertfordshire, in August 1943. Why Hitchin? I never found out. The second mystery factor was the date on my birth certificate: 1944. Odd or what?

There was a lot going on!

My late grandmother described my first witnessing of anything associated with the war: a German jet-assisted bomb called a Doodlebug. A low humming noise accompanied its predetermined journey, which cut off before suddenly dipping earthbound to explode in fields near Mancroft Towers, next to the Norwich railway line. (I was in my pram looking out through an upstairs front bedroom window.)

Another brief incident surprised Gran, who was hanging out washing in the backyard and witnessed airmen waving from within the plane before bombing Lake Lothing, then heading out into the North Sea.

There was no time to be pushed into the Anderson shelter. The brief intrusion lasted only seconds.

Our first home was a top-floor flat in Crown Street, adjoining the Town Hall buildings. It proved not to be suitable for a baby, and both grandparents suggested we live with them until something else came along.

Number Two Canary Cottage (28 Whapload Road), opposite Christ Church, was a semi-detached, cramped, sub-standard home for four persons: Robert William and wife Catherine Harriet, daughter Barbara, and myself. The sea, being only a couple of hundred yards from where we lived, was the backdrop of my earliest years. I could hear it constantly from my bedroom, rattling the pathetically thin downstairs windows while sounds of screeching bees came from under the gaps of the front door. I often sat on the bottom step of the stairs and listened for ages, dreaming of faraway countries with sunshine and donkey carts, sandy beaches, and ice cream.

I was ten years old when the great floods of 1953 created severe damage and loss of life from Norfolk to Essex.

We were asleep when the water brought all kinds of damage to the community. We were flooded to a depth of three feet four inches in our house. This awful force of nature brought about the mass abandonment of what was called The Beach, containing fishermen's families, including grandparents, who had gone to sea to earn a pittance they called wages, living in unheated, squalid, unlit homes. The sea was known as "the widow maker," and over the years, brothers, fathers, uncles, and nephews never returned from attempting to make a living from the sea. It was ironic. The sea could supply but also take back, as if life were a loan!

Father

Robert William (Bobby) Day was a short (five-foot-one), blue-eyed, blonde, well-read, knowledgeable man who would appear from a sea-going trip without having a shave for whatever period it had been, throw down his ex-naval kitbag full of dirty clothes, poke his head into the kitchen where we usually sat, get kissed by his stubbly whiskers, then say, "Going to the Bethel for a bath and a mug of hot sweet tea." We wouldn't see him for at least two hours and would be much happier under the influence of drink.

He went to sea at fourteen years old because it was the thing to do at a time when drifter fishing (then trawling) was the only employment in the area. He didn't have a holiday ashore after the herring season but applied for agency work, which meant we wouldn't see him for months on end.

On one trip to Norway, he worked on a whaling ship and explained it was the best-paid but most sickening (literally). The giant beasts were hauled up the open rear of the factory ship and sliced into sections with long, sharp machete-type knives on extended poles.

The gang of men trod in blood and entrails, which made them retch and throw up where they stood. Everything had commercial usage, including the production of margarine and perfume. The Chinese were the main customers.

Currently, lots of towns have abandoned the fishing tradition. When Dad was earning, there were Buckie, Aberdeen, Banff, Peterhead and Fraserburgh in Scotland, and South Shields, Hull, Grimsby, Great Yarmouth, Newquay, Holyhead and Rye in England. Herring was big business in those days.

On another eight-month voyage (icebreaking), he went to Russia and had to wear anti-glare glasses because of the vast, as-far-as-the-eye-can-see whiteness of the ice-packed seascape, but he never talked about what he did. He was a small man, but certainly had a huge quest for travel.

He worked on colliers, huge filthy coal transporter ships from Poland and Germany. When he came home, Barbara and I squeezed his cheeks, nose and chin to get rid of the horrible, ingrained dirt in his pores. By the time we finished, he looked as though he had been sunbathing. A couple of quick head-ducks in a bucket of cold water soon cleared the muck away! When he first met Mother, he worked on dredges, clearing canals and waterways, embankments and shallow rivers.

He did many trips on coasters belonging to F. T. Everard & Company in Kent, with names ending in -ity. Examples: Clarity, Spontaneity, etc., with commercial fuel being the freight. Father died at sea off the coast of Brixham, aged thirty-six, from lung complications.

He rolled his own ciggies, but when he had money, bought Senior Service, although Woodbines were cheaper.

As an artist, he painted oils onto scallop shells: sloops, brigantines, schooners, galleons and Nordic decorative vessels. One horrific habit we witnessed was that he cut his toenails with a single-edged razor blade.

I was fourteen when he left us and never got to know him as land-based children share with their fathers. He went on a sea trip but never returned. Mother gave me two shillings: "You don't want to see his coffin, go to the pictures (cinema) and have an ice-cream." To which I had to obey! She never seemed to be happy in her lifetime. A real shame.

Father tried to relax the only way fishermen could: by going to pubs with their mates and getting the previous week's harsh, sometimes hazardous, sea voyage out of their minds by consuming large amounts of beer. This caused lots of unusual incidents with meals left in the oven. We were never told that he had an operation that involved a metal plate being inserted into his skull, and this triggered a change in our Dad's behaviour, which frightened us.

More than once, we saw him throw his late lunch across one side of the room to the other and watched food dribble down the green-painted wall; it might have looked amusing, but it was far from funny. Barbara and I held on to each other, stopped eating, and went into the tiny, dark kitchen, out of the way of what happened. There were also a few times I got between him and Mother to prevent her from being punched and grabbed hold of. We were scared!

For reasons known only to Mother, she never trusted our beloved Dad. He would smile while she questioned him and told her to "stop being like a bloody policeman", then walked into the rear yard and had a smoke.

I was very young, but I always thought a lot about him. I enjoyed the few times he took me to meet mates who were night watchmen on drifters.

I had to hold on and descend a metal ladder (going backwards) fifteen feet to the deck below. It was quite a challenge, but the anticipation of going aboard eased my mind. It was exciting and a new experience for my innocent upbringing. Anything to get out of the house from constant bickering was fine by me.

Mother

Looking much older than her actual age, she was tiny, with skeletal arms, but had the strength of a Greek warrior and did the best she could, looking after the home and caring for two children on her own. It must have been difficult.

Mother was a strict disciplinarian, especially towards me. For the slightest hiccup, she would readily give an ear tweak or a quick slap to the back of my legs… "Don't do that again."

She rarely smiled unless a neighbour called in to chat or cadge something, then a magical appearance of a cake or a Swiss roll, which disappeared as soon as the neighbour left. Barbara and I seldom shared anything with a visitor.

Mother could be mean. Many a time, I was sent to bed early for not being at home by a certain time, or had wet shoes and socks from an unplanned search for crabs under the pier head.

She lived on "old wives' tales" and superstitions. If it poured with rain and thundered, she closed the curtains, turned mirrors against the wall and made sure all knives were shut away in the kitchen drawer. If we were out walking and saw a nun, we had to cross over to the other side of the road. It was bad luck. When an alarm-blaring ambulance sped down the street, "someone has died from an accident."

If salt was spilt, she had to pick up a few grains and throw them over her left shoulder, another symbolic gesture. One peculiar saying was: "If a teaspoon fell to the floor, a baby had been born." It was annoying living with stupid sayings, which ruled her life. Daft.

Eating together and knives touching in an X meant: "There's going to be an argument in the house." It was really maddening. I hated it!

There were no photographs of their wedding, which was another enigma. They never talked about how she met Dad, nothing like that. They rowed continuously. There were times Mother was deliberately argumentative to create unpleasantness, egg him on with her suspicious questions. Why? We did not know at that tender age.

She died from bowel cancer aged 77. Our diminutive, nervy, cleaning Mother. Buried with Dad in Lowestoft cemetery.

I never knew where she originated from, but Father was a local man.

There were several similar outbursts that could give a wrong image of our parents and would be unfair and unsympathetic.

One eye-opening fact was that she smoked perfumed continental cigarettes with a title (not sure), Spanish Shores. Sold in tins. It must have been when she was a young woman because the one employment mentioned (a trainee nurse later confirmed as a cleaner) was in a hospital in Basingstoke, Hampshire.

Sister Barbara

Born in one of the guesthouses (previously a private nursing home) opposite Kensington Gardens, Barbara June was seven years my junior. I remember taking a box of Meltis jelly sweets for Mother and peering into the bedside cot, pointing: "My new sister looks like a tiny monkey." Some babies did!

Dad would call us early Saturday evening, from wherever he was. We had to walk a few hundred yards to the nearest telephone kiosk, next door to the popular little café across the docks.

It was amazing to us youngsters to hear his voice coming from Scotland or Holland, with his usual: "Hello, blondie-blue-eyes, are you being a good girl for mummy?" and a similar brief: "You be a good boy" for me, leaving Mother with a few remaining seconds to reply. Nearby was the large open space of the Eastern Counties Bus Terminal, where, in summer months, buses and coaches from all over the UK would stop and allow passengers to disembark for a break and a wee. (Nearby underground toilets.)

Barbara survived all the illnesses every young girl went through, but later in life, a thyroid problem caused recurring suffering, and she became overweight. Her legs enlarged to an extent she could hardly walk or stand. She had to have a hospital bed installed but never improved health-wise, culminating in having a shunt—delicate wiring into the brain—to relieve pressure and constant pain.

Over the years, she was an avid Skoda member, and with her husband David, made frequent trips to outings and rallies with their small caravan, home and abroad. She became a committee member, then a treasurer. Serious illness prevailed, eventually going blind, bedridden and deaf. She died in her sleep in her sixties.

Attempting to learn more about Mother and Father by asking other relatives was a no-go, as if something that had occurred in the past had to be kept secret.

Grandfather Knights died and was buried two weeks before I was notified of his passing. This upset me, and I didn't contact my mother for ages. One comment from an undisclosed member of the family (another secrecy?) was that he, Grandfather, wanted to "tell John something." What was it, I wonder?

Every family, so the saying goes, "has a skeleton in their cupboard," perhaps appropriate to my background, but I will never know!

Early Memories

Initial biographical recollections were eye-opening circumstances for an innocent lad whose prior travels were limited to Norwich or Great Yarmouth before going to London to see Queen Elizabeth II's coronation decorations. Seeing buildings on postcards or television, if you were lucky enough to have one in your home, was incredibly exciting. Schoolmates jumped up and down when spotting St. Paul's Cathedral, the Houses of Parliament, 10 Downing Street, Buckingham Palace, and Marble Arch. Girls screamed and made jumping, dancing movements. It was a wonderful day out and will be recalled throughout our lifetime. Trafalgar Square was a battlefield, walking on the pigeon-poo-spattered ground, trying to dodge the shitting, diving birds, finding shoulders to sit on or pose with other nervously watching strangers. It was horribly slippery underfoot. On the return journey by steam train from Liverpool Street station, I got smuts in my eyes, looking out from an open window, from the smoke and steam coming through the Ipswich railway tunnel. For us pre-teens, it would be a talking point for ages.

We had to save one shilling every week to pay for the unique trip, and remember it cost one pound two-and-sixpence, which was a lot of pennies in those long-ago times. We never had pocket money.

Each train journey was a joyous, exciting time. The sound of the train wheels going over the rails made rhythmic clickety-click-clickety-click sounds, and listening to the repetitive musical notes, you could easily get mesmerised and fall asleep. In each carriage, a distinctive cloth smell came from deep-red patterned seats. Having any luggage, you placed it above where you sat and well within reach if you tiptoed. Six people could be seated in each compartment. It was lovely in winter when a heater beneath the seats kept things comfortably warm. Two railway fans accompanied me to Great Yarmouth, and we stayed on the station to watch a 'Namer' engine come in with masses of special day-out tourists from York. My small notebook had names and numbers of all rolling stock which were doing the rounds, but it is long gone and lost. How thrilled we were as whatever it was hissed, steamed, and clanked its entrance into the echoing space, and the din from the outpouring passengers was something else — not as loud as a football match, but not far off! The engine might have been an A5 locomotive because I recall it was bright blue.

On another special sighting, a rare appearance of a 2-10-10-2 pulled four brake vans and slowly passed with hardly a sound. It was from 'up north' and a stranger to our region. A real monster locomotive of great pulling power.

Shunting on British Railways' property, two square-shaped black-painted Y2/Y3 engines endlessly huffed and puffed, carrying (pulling) tons of sand and gravel, from within a noisy, rattling Victorian wooden tower excavation structure next to the old seawall, towards the old extension, whose strong, weathered, ancient oak thick legs were embedded in seawater.

Most recollections are from decades ago when I had a full head of hair, excellent hearing, didn't wear spectacles, and owned strong, gleaming white, toothy pegs, without prostate annoyance or gradual memory loss. Nowadays, it is a distinctly different world from when people were more polite, caring, considerate, and helpful, without available benefits to hardship cases. We had more than enough hardships, as all older people will relate! Today's generations wouldn't be able to cope and exist as their grandparents had to, but that's life, I suppose.

It feels as though everyone is in a constant state of hurrying, and if a casual "Good day," interrupts their progress, you may get a smile in return.

I once said it to a guy who stopped, turned around, and asked, "Do I know you?"

All my employments involved the public, and an everyday polite greeting with a smile seemed appropriate to be friendly. Was I wrong?

I talked to all walks of life; it is a natural, built-in attitude I adopted. Politeness doesn't cost anything, but to some, it is a confrontational situation. Never mind. I am too long in the tooth to take umbrage; it's my way!

Childhood and Education

I was excused from most schools' games because of a "weak chest" resulting from bronchitis as a baby, leaving an asthmatic, freckled-faced, brown-eyed lad who attempted playing rugby. Being small was ideal when a scrum was needed, but never appreciated being grabbed by the testicles, bitten on the neck, or heavy sweating bodies crushing me into cold grass, and being hoisted in the air was another brief shock. I was never interested in athletics, purely for the reason that I quickly got out of breath. It would have been smashing to have won a race—or be awarded a cup or a shield! I would have loved to see how far I could have run! Somehow, my breathing improved through cross-country running. The course bordered a large open park area, a cemetery, tarmac roads, and up a steep incline, arriving back at school gates. I enjoyed splashing through muddy puddles but hated the showers, which were either scalding hot or freezing cold.

I was in the Faraday class, which was yellow. Others were Caxton, Stephenson, and Newton. Loved Geography, but anything to do with arithmetic was abysmal; I had a mental blockage. It's a blindness of sorts. Always had it.

I can easily cock up drinks orders in reciprocal socialising. Useless at mental maths and only succeeded in reading up to the twelve-times multiplication table.

I was never bullied, threatened, or hit for no apparent reason. Some lads were. I stayed for school lunches, which I thoroughly enjoyed, strange as it may seem. Liked semolina, sago, and tapioca—yummy.

Missed sitting O levels. Asthma kept me at home. Did them later, but according to the person reading my results, I had written far too much. Left the secondary modern boys' school in July 1958, not quite fifteen years old. And never been kissed! Whoop de doh.

Leaving school was just another day. I was told that a plaster-of-Paris polar bear I sculpted was to be on display in the Regent Road art studio.

A metal poker is still within my shed, likewise a G-clamp, red paint gleaming in all its glory.

Don't know if a special gift of a metal weathervane currently abides within the rear garden of 41, The Street, Corton. I made a short-legged wooden stool for my mother, which she kept in her kitchen on Lorne Park Road. But the small aluminium towel and soap dish vanished into the ether. All made during metal and woodwork lessons.

No "leaving school" celebrations were presented. No free food. Sweet Fanny Adams. The day I left school was very un-special!

The only job I had was a shop assistant in what was called a general store, which sold everything from toothpaste to lawnmowers, paraffin and soap powders, bedding, cutlery and crockery, pots and pans, and bicycles. My first chore each morning was to lay out lots of products on artificial grass to attract passing pedestrians. Slow-selling items became "Sales Prices" with knocked-down discounts accordingly.

Metal wheelbarrows glinted in the morning sunlight. Brooms stood to attention, toilet rolls became items of convenience, and rolls of lino needed laying. Lots of passers-by smiled and said "good morning," which I liked.

Bagging up and individually pricing innumerable quantities of bulb fibre was one hellishly boring, repetitive task. A pile of it was delivered overnight. Heaven only knows how many bags I filled and priced: 2 lb… 5 lb… 10 lb… twirled the plastic bags and wrapped a sticky orange label on each neck. Did this for four consecutive days without leaving the premises; the smell started making me sneeze, which was worrying. That's all I wanted.

One afternoon, I had to load a carpet onto the crossbar of a trade bike, which had a smaller front wheel than the normal-sized rear wheel. Did what I was told, took my time, and with white prickly twine, tied the heavy object to the crossbar. Because of its bulk, keeping the steering straight ahead was difficult.

The seat was uncomfortable, to say the least. The delivery address was three miles away. At least the return journey would be easier, as it meant a downhill, feet-off-pedals ride. If I took my time, I would be back just before knocking off for the day.

I would walk across the bridge which separated the south of the town from the north, then pedal the ascending roadway. That was my plan.

Hadn't gone far, perhaps a couple of hundred yards, when the damn carpet started unwrapping itself. I wobbled, trying to control the movement. Car horns hooted, cycle bells jingled, and a double-decker council bus was not far behind me. I was causing a traffic holdup; what could I do?

Eventually, over the busy bridge, a traffic police officer directing the flow of motor vehicles waved in my direction. The look on his reddening face was not that of friendly conversation. My journey was about to be stopped before it began. Bugger.

He took his time looking round the bike, which had seen better days. Felt the tyres, applied the squeaky brakes, obviously intent on finding faults on the machine. He wrote notes on his little pad, put it in his top pocket, wiped sweat from his forehead, and said, "I've taken details of the bike, and your manager will be warned about what happened. Don't they have a van for deliveries?" I never said a thing. Just looked dumb.

That employment lasted five weeks. I got fed up doing the same things every day. I never got to know the older male members of staff. They were full of themselves and never once helped the other assistants. All of them smoked, and the male restroom reeked. I loathed the smell.

Living only a few hundred yards from the seawall defences and an elevated coastguard hut, the sea could be heard crashing against the old barricade of rocks and boulders like an approaching thunderstorm.

Standing on my bed, I could see the highest waves. If lying across it, my head would touch one wall and my feet would be against the other. There was nothing else in the room.

In winter, when November showers and gale-force winds attacked the house, noises like angry bees came from a gap under the front door. Things called dogs were old sheets, stuffed with blankets and socks, and wedged tightly against the gap. We had to do the same thing to the other doors.

I stayed with my adorable grandparents at every available time I could. In fact, they were the most important part of my growing up, and I never knew why, but they looked after me more than my mother. I cried after staying with them during the summer holidays.

Grandfather had been in the First World War, and seeing photographs, he drove mules and horses carrying massive guns on wooden carriages with huge metal wheels through deep, clinging mud up to the knees and axle level.

On his death, in their bedroom, in a corner cupboard, was a superb example of a colourful uniform. A magnificent helmet with a white feathered plume, navy blue trousers with a wide red band from waist to trouser bottoms, a red three-quarter-length tunic, a multi-coloured cummerbund around the waist, shiny thigh-high black leather riding boots with jingling spurs strapped to the heels, and a sword wrapped in its scabbard in layers of tissue paper. Completing the outfit was a "Sam Brown", a leather shoulder holster for a handgun. All highly polished; it must have looked magnificent when hundreds of soldiers were on parade astride their horses.

These items, along with lots of mantelpiece decorations and souvenirs from holiday trips, vanished remarkably quickly from the house. Dressing tables with hairbrushes, combs, and scent sprays went the same way. I found lots of picture frames smashed against the coal shed wall. A selfish, non-caring attitude to once-cherished items owned by senior members of the family—how awful.

Grandfather knew a man who hired rowing boats. He surprised me one afternoon by asking if I wanted to go fishing. I nearly wet myself with instant excitement. Modern health and safety factors would be shocked to learn of a twelve-year-old skinny kid going out in a rowing boat by himself, fishing on a Broad. Another example of yesteryear's nonchalant attitude, but it was marvellous for someone so young, without a care in his life, doing what he wanted to do. I learnt to row and scull by watching my grandfather do it.

There are many moments I could willingly recall, but this is not purely an autobiography and might become too sentimental or one-sided. My aim is to give tasters of what my younger years contained and the experiences I happily and innocently went through. I adored my grandparents; they helped me no end. Both are buried in St. Faith's Cemetery, Norwich. Bless them: Lily and Ernest Albert Knights. RIP.

Creative Pursuits and Literary Work

One aspect of school stuck out from the usual. On a Friday afternoon, which was a free period from lessons, a teacher suggested reading from a chosen book, which was a surprise to the class. It was unusually enjoyable, and each speaker got a round of applause from classmates. I cannot recall how or why, but I picked up a book containing poetry and recited quite a long piece of prose. That was the very first time I heard poetry, and not until my thirties did I choose to read Sir John Betjeman, wartime poets, Philip Larkin, and other popular writers, absorbing their words instead of instantly forgetting what was just read. Descriptions became more vivid images in my mind, and I began writing them myself. This gradually increased to become an everyday part of my life. I am seldom away from the "creative machine", reworking stuff from forty years ago. I'm addicted, but there are other aspects of creation I pursue and challenge.

I compose light-hearted verse as well as "serious" works, so readers are not bored with subject content, and I attempt documentary-type descriptions that conjure imaginary pictures within the text. Views of particularly picturesque beauty tempt my craving to look down and compose. Music does the same. Admiring paintings can set me off, and buildings too. I suppose it's to do with an inner sympathetic concern, whatever. Thinking about those who built, composed, or painted, I appreciate that sort of thing!

One mild rhyme heard from grown-ups was to do with toilets. Coincidentally, decades later, I would be employed in an occupation within public conveniences—irony, or what?

It was associated with having to pay a penny coin into a brass box attached to a toilet door, which opened as the penny dropped. The adage to 'spend a penny' was apt. I don't know if folk say it nowadays.

The wording was:

"Here I sit broken-hearted,

Paid my penny but only farted."

To a young, innocent lad, this was rude… haven't times changed?

I am not a technically adept person and keep my writing as simple as possible without using complicated words to emphasise or add an alternative "long word." Iambic pentameters sound like an electricity term to me. As a writer, I seldom read, which caused open-mouthed stares or lowering of jaws in disbelief: "You don't read—how extraordinary!" or "Good grief!"

I get to page forty and my eyes droop from concentration, so I stop; otherwise, I would doze off with the book still in my hands. My last book was by Jeremy Clarkson about his farm—a good read with lots of funny bits. There is a PS reference to reading on the last page. I also have *Confessions of a Bookseller*, ready to peruse.

Some quirky, quaint quips may be familiar. Many might not have been heard of in years. Humour is within the text content, and I sincerely hope there is something for everybody.

Two tortoises are walking on a beach. One says:

"Why are you trembling?"

The reply was:

"It's shell shock."

"Why did the tornado suddenly stop at Newcastle?"

"It was out-of-breath."

According to road safety statistics, one person gets knocked down every twelve seconds.

AND IS THOROUGHLY ANNOYED ABOUT IT.

I Wonder How Loneliness Grows?

(From listening to a record)

Does loneliness start from today or tomorrow?

From heartache, upset, or terrible sorrow,

Does it fly up and bite off your nose?

I wonder how loneliness grows.

Does loneliness grow from a hint or a token,

Or can it be started from a spiteful word spoken?

Maybe it clings to your clothes.

I wonder how loneliness grows.

Can selfishness cancel a yearned-for emotion

That sincerely seeks love with respect and devotion,

When sentiment and care surely show?

I wonder how loneliness can grow.

Can choosing a loved one become so demanding,

As bitterness festers with a power so alarming,

And resentment is cold as icefloes?

I wonder how loneliness grows.

Can emptiness be brushed as patterned wallpaper,

Brightness eludes one intentional escaper,

And hatred splashes on fingers and toes...

I wonder how loneliness grows?

"Have your eyes been checked?"

"No, they've always been blue."

~ Anon

"Memory and teeth grow weaker with time."

~ Anon

"I'm not under the influence of inkahol that some thinkle peep."

~ Anon

The mice that live in the attic room are always out for a laugh.

They get their kicks on Saturday nights watching busty Mrs Grant in her bath.

The Dip

Once the freezing-cold, breath-showing early morning mist finally ebbs, I scan the spacious playing area we young kids scrambled on, jumped over, cycled madly to the dunes, and threw stones into the pond's mirror-like water to break the stillness. Wooden seats, where teenage kisses were tested, are still there; what tales they could tell! While in summer, bodies sprawled and got sunburnt from falling asleep in the comforting heat.

Grown-ups appeared with noisy, excited children. Three ever-yapping dogs crazily chased tails and leapt to catch balloons, Frisbees, or frail-looking balsa planes. Picnic hampers with ginger beer, Vimto, crisps, and cartons of trifle for afters saw daylight. Adults drank wine instead of pop and preferred sandwiches to hula-hoops.

Hordes of yelling, spitting, chewing-gum youths lingered until bored, then vacated the area.

Large, stooping trees were challenges to older boy daredevils, while mums and dads shouted warnings and told kids not to go too far away.

Allotments are still there, but no old-age pipe-smokers work near run-down sheds.

Before leaving, yours truly stood in dogshit… is it all worth it?

This area was in local news because of morons burning brand-new seats and tables near a children's play area. No offenders were caught, but the council was advised to trim bushes to head height, lop off loosely hanging low branches, and remove wooden fencing. More facilities were added that couldn't be removed. Metal seats and tables were firmly concreted, replacing the charred remains.

Pathways were widened, and trespassing notices were glued to nearby lampposts. However, it's still a favourite meeting place for dog lovers.

There were brief worries concerning youngsters being bothered by loitering men, but the two people apprehended came from Great Yarmouth and received prison sentences due to repeated harassment incidents. Swans with their cygnets now leisurely glide amongst the greenery, which needs clearing.

I Don't Want to Die Wearing Pyjamas

I don't want to die wearing pyjamas, comfortably warm in a sheet.

Prefer being out in the country where grass and moss tickle my feet.

I would like to hear my childhood sea gently lapping over my toes.

Feel the strength of gale-force wind when snot dribbled down my nose.

I would smile at the wonderful sunrise, gladly kiss clouds goodbye.

Be caressed by sweltering summer heat, hear gulls in a clear blue sky.

Fresh air, the sea, bird sounds, nothing else compares.

I don't wish to die in pyjamas or fall down any steep, bloody stairs.

I visited scenic beauty, including Scotland's panoramas.

Swum (only a few shivering minutes) in Cardigan Bay

but would loathe dying wearing pyjamas.

As a youngster, I adored all animals. Camels, elephants, and llamas.

Almost got trodden on by a Rhea. My wish? Not to die in pyjamas.

Forestry, coolness, fruit were always refreshing,

fizzy drinks, lollypops, ice cream with chopped bananas

Loved nature's display, fishing on The Broads all day

but would hate to die wearing pyjamas.

I have written science fiction to imagine a futuristic scenario where democracy is history, and anarchy rules. No police force, only a security militia. Food is scarce due to world-governing embargoes. Immigration problems revert to being sent to lunar locations. Hospitals are run by military staff, with a controversial offshore installation for non-curable diseases. And it's worrying… very worrying.

Whispering Danger

Did you hear that subdued talking?

Could you detect a creaking stair?

Was it someone downstairs walking?

Did you sense fear in the air?

Was the sound incredibly awful

of crying babies, screaming kids.

Taken away and placed in bins

and hidden by tight-fitting lids.

Did you see any darkened figures,

hurrying past the crowded stores.

Throwing petrol bombs through windows

and if open shop front doors

Current news is seldom happy,

death and bombings, suicide pacts

When can ever Peace be on offer,

when is the time for all to relax?

R U Aware?

There's a glow in the snow. Can you see it to the left of those tall pine trees? Beyond the valley and lake, there, where grass grows up to your knees.

There's a fear in the air. Can you feel a sense of foreboding, a threat? After a thunderstorm is over, when everything's soaking wet.

There's a birth on Earth. Can you sense it? No cries bear witness to pain, a distant humming pulse that throbs, like an invisible, slow-moving train.

There's a smell on the feel of flowers, a pleasant, heady perfume not from aerosol spray cans, a natural, healthy bloom.

There's a prize in the skies. Can you win it? You don't need to enter a race. Something mind-boggling happens, but you must wear a smile on your face.

There's free food on the road. Are you hungry? A claim must be made in full by an unbiased, serious businessperson straddling an irate charging bull.

There's a wall ten feet tall. Can you climb it? Without a ladder or frame, put plans to paper, be an escaper and pray that it doesn't pour with rain.

There's something not quite right. Can you see it? Passed piles of skeletons burnt black, beyond mass graves and freezing curling waves, of man's INHUMANITY and there's no turning back.

"What are all goldfish called… BOB?" (Have to think about that?)

Quirky Quaint Quips

There are no chapters within this cryptic publication, which was created to bring prose and obscure text forward to relax an "elitist snobbery" of rhyme-folk labelled arty-farty, only for ex-university scholastic types. This is not true, dear reader. I did not attend such establishments to be better than Tommy down the road (apologies to Tommy) and have written inane articles for fifty years, mainly for posterity factors.

I WRITE ABOUT EVERYTHING, praying one day it will be worth the hours of selecting reams of dubious, nay silly, sayings from the past, to bring smiles to those who might not have heard of weird or bizarre writing. Using modern phraseology, they are RETRO amusement.

I could have extricated lots of children's school-day rhymes, although a few are within. The majority of the wording of this barmy publication is from the fathomless, unfettered imagination I have owned since birth. There are cellars deep within the dungeon of creativity, but I have not got the key to their doors.

Here We Go Then…

Leaving a secondary modern boys' school in the late nineteen-fifties without qualifications, I took on a shop assistant's position in a store before enlisting in the Royal Air Force Boy Entrants Training at Cosford, where I became a qualified cook within Bulk Catering Management. Eighteen months of serious studying combined with practical tutoring from former chefs. Daunting indeed.

If today's generation requires bespoke knowledge of numerous trades, enter one of our military services to do just that. They thoroughly educate, discipline, and qualify you to exacting standards. Adventure is inclusive of a force's regime, but there are tough challenges, lots of demands to fulfil without assistance from parents, which, to most youngsters, was the most severe of all considerations.

From experience, I saw young men openly cry themselves to sleep, and two days after joining up, would apply for 'discharge by purchase.' The worst single act that caused further upset and more tears was wrapping civilian clothes into a bundle, shoes and all, addressing labels to your home, and waxing knots to retain content. Emotional indeed. No civvies now!

All three military services are ideal outlets to seek a trade, make friends for life, see the world, and become better people than you were prior to the rigours of service life… chase that dream, have an adventure… go for it!

English was my most rewarding of school subjects, likewise geography, but I was beyond hope with arithmetic. Never got past page one of algebra. It might as well have been a foreign language. I was useless. There was, and still is, a missing component in my grey matter with anything to do with methodical formulae. Cannot play cards at all. Easily can cock up a drinks order during reciprocal socialising. Along with remembering people's names, which is another issue. I have an excellent memory for a brief time!

But I can recall an event from early childhood in the wink of an eye.

Lots of ideas brought to life were from dreams and instantly scribbled down into a notebook on a bedside locker. Creative spasms quickly subside and disappear, never to be retrieved. This is too true.

According to foreign students, English is the hardest language to learn because there are many descriptives that sound the same and require further explanation, for example, where… wear… ware… fair… fare… fear, etc.

Quirky Quaint Quips is unusual among publications as it is "not normal" in content. Humour has a curative, therapeutic value to tickle chuckle muscles and be amusing, but the contents should not be taken too seriously. (Only joshin, a Norfolk word.)

Slaved away on an ancient tower PC, caressing the keys as quickly as my wobbly fingers could, with the sole intention of making light once again of the former dark years of COVID-19, and bring smiles to faces that endured more pain and sadness than I experienced writing this. Expletives and sexual innuendoes are scattered throughout purely for effect, not to cause undue unpleasantness. Would never do that.

It's only the hairs on a gooseberry that stop it from being a grape.

How Hi is a Chinese man…. Yes. I know he is.

On the other hand, a thumb and four fingers.

Get off the gas stove, Granny, you're too old to ride the range.

Sign in a closing shop window:

"Bridegroom's wedding suit For Sale... trousers have been let-down."

What's the difference between a dirty mat and a bottle of medicine?

One is taken up and shaken, the other is shaken up and taken.

The world is full of willing people... those that are willing to work and those that are willing to let them.

Smile awhile, and when you smile, others smile, and soon there're miles and miles of smiles, and life's worthwhile because you smile.

I'm not a complete idiot... there are bits missing.

Three deep holes in the ground... WELL WELL WELL.

Two ants crawling across the head of a bald man were mates. One said to the other: "I knew this area when it was a short-cut."

If you fall off that wall and break your leg, don't come running to me.

Two flies sat on a breakfast cereal box top. One said:

"Why are you out of breath?"

The older fly gasped: "It says tear around the dotted line."

How do you know an elephant has pinched food from the 'fridge'?

There are footprints in the custard.

A young girl walks into a classroom and sits down at her desk.

The teacher asks:

"What is that dreadful smell, Maisie?"

The girl replies:

"A kipper, miss."

"Why do you wear a kipper?"

"'I want to smell like my older sister."

On Thursday, I slid down a greasy pole... he was not amused... (hope this does not create any racial friction)

Highs and lows for children and clowns...

... see-saws have their ups and downs.

"It's truly a beautiful bright sunny day," said Simon to his friend Joe Tree.

"I hope it's nice tomorrow as well, I'm going to the moon for tea.'

I witnessed something magical yesterday... two HGV lorries turned into a lay-by.

If pigs could fly... bacon would go up.

Do you know the difference between an elephant's backside and a letter box?

If the answer is NO... "I won't ask you to post my letters, matey."

I have never been to a giant bird sale or seen any heavy plant crossing.

What's the difference between a heavy woman and an ocean? Weight and sea.

Is it true you have a poor memory... reply immediately... A poor what?

What is good for water on the brain?

A Tap on the Knee

"Where are your buccaneers?"

"On each side of my bucking-head."

Camel's spit,

bird's shit,

a dead body found in the grass.

TV crews reporting news. A police officer scratching his arse.

An almighty smell reeking like hell encourages flies to squat.

Hose pipes wrongly connected, instead of icy water IT'S HOT.

Beautiful peacocks lost all their feathers, now squeak, whistle and squawk,

giant fish covered in putrid slime, scared old ladies on their afternoon walk.

Frogs wearing top hats and tails welcomed guests from abroad,

whilst frantic dancing, enormous naked fat ladies were totally ignored.

Why doesn't the Pope have a bath?
He never looks down on the unemployed!

Music was provided by tiny white mice playing drums, guitar, and flute.

Dressed in matching hound-tooth jackets, they looked endearingly cute.

Bees and butterflies go to parties wearing their best clothes,

but later feel regretfully sorry for the partners they drunkenly chose.

What's the difference between a fart and a sneeze...

a sneeze has not been through any s**t.

A constipated mathematician developed chronic constipation

but finally worked it out with a pencil.

Old eyes twinkle, slow arms heavy to raise, tired feet in well-worn slippers,

can no longer enjoy a rare sirloin steak, and make do with a couple of

kippers.

Two gay Scots, Ben Doone and Phil McCracken,
shared a luxury apartment with David Fitzgerald and Paul
Fitzmaurice.

I talk to the trees... that's why they put me away!

A sign above a Norwich Ford Garage customer reception area states:

IN GOD WE TRUST OTHERS PAY CASH

Bodgy Todds came through the mail
'cos The China Sea was unsafe to sail.
Blimrods with Crusties were annoyed getting wet
and blamed it all on a young girl called Claudette.

HAIR TODAY... Bald tomorrow

A family of fleas on holiday
were so happy they jumped for Joy...
for Anne, Mr and Mrs Smith and their dog,
the vicar's wife, a postman!

A well-known granny from Taunton always wore decorative glasses.

A most surprising fact about her is that she's a model in life-drawing classes.

Whether the weather is fine, whether the weather is hot,

we'll, whatever the weather, whether we like it or not.

I had a little nut tree.

Nothing would it bear but a single nutmeg and a golden pear. The King of Spain's daughter came to visit me,

all for the sake of my little nut tree.

Knickerless girls should never climb trees or do handstands against a wall.

If I said you had a beautiful body, would you hold it against me?

"That's a good idea, son," (Max Bygraves), Radio broadcaster, 1950s Singer.

"Didn't he do well?" (Bruce Forsyth) Compere.

"Shut that door," (Larry Grayson), Comedian.

"Hello, my darlings" (Charlie Drake).

Ronnie

Ronnie the rat wore a bright yellow hat,

as well as standing he sometimes sat.

Played a guitar and could also whistle.

Strummed the strings with a prickly thistle.

He stole wheels off cycles and burgled houses,

and was once arrested for dropping his trousers.

Had a young girlfriend, Louise Boulders,

who carried little Ronnie on her big, broad shoulders.

They jumped off a pier-head... she wore no clothes,

Ronnie was fine, but Louise broke her nose.

A young girl asked her mother...

"Mummy, why are your hands so soft and smooth?"

"Daddy does all the washing-up, dear."

There was a young lady from Leeds who swallowed a packet of seeds

out of her bum a geranium come... her lady garden grew all the weeds.

It is not the cough that carries you off, it's the coffin they carry you off in.

Was going to send you a fiver but had stuck down the envelope.

Must go now. There's a horrible smell in the kitchen

coming from your loving mother.

A young married lady from Rainham,

all photos with paint she would spray 'em

her children unruly would laugh at her cruelly

she'd pick up a broom and then brain 'em.

Jack and Jill went up the hill to fetch a pail of water.

Jill came down with half-a-crown, but it was not for fetching water.

An Indian Fakir named Rahsee,

could bend himself double quite easily.

Aesthetic it would be, uncomfortable should be.

Never tries it when coughing or wheezy.

The easiest thing to do if you cannot get to sleep is lay on the very

edge of the bed... you will soon drop off.

There's a hole in the mattress... so I will see you in the spring.

"I'm a good little mummy's boy. I don't swear."

"S**t Bugger Arseholes… I don't care."

She was only a tobacconist's daughter but was the absolute best shag

in the shop.

What are baby caterpillars called? KITTEN PILLARS (of course)

What do you call forty-six-inch breasts? Wonderful gifts of nature.

A young maiden with brown hair and eyes was enormous, a terrible

size

twenty-odd stone and still not full-grown,

she could crack coconuts in her thighs.

If all the females lived over the sea,

what a wonderful swimmer I would be.

"Alternative Menu's."

Composed 2024.

All potatoes have been roasted, lots of grilled sausages too,

What did they do, I wonder? Will the bars be open at the zoo?

Cream splits got their treatments at last. Bakewell Tarts attend deportment

classes.

Bath buns no longer taste of soap. Blind beans and macaroni wear glasses.

Danish pastries surrendered their passports. Swiss cheeses cannot yodel

after dark.

Chelsea Buns joined Fulham FC. Cucumber sandwiches are banned from

the park.

Sausage rolls are prevented from frightening dogs and cats.

Omelettes, along with pie and mash, won a contract for Alpington Flats.

Bread and butter puddings got engaged to knives and forks.

Made friends with Italian meringues. They go for long Sunday walks.

Yorkshire puddings and Jersey spuds were friendly with Gretna Greens.

Welsh rabbits had to cut their hair. You should have heard their screams.

Black Forest gateau had trees cut down. Apple crumbles finally collapsed.

Chuck steaks flew across the room and landed in pensioners' laps.

Trifles became important. Rare steaks can be seen everywhere.

Mock Turtle Soup is now the genuine stuff, and there's a menu under each

person's chair.

Gravy is served in miniature milk churns, sufficient to cover the meat.

Bubble and squeak is served twice a week. Foreign chiropodists admitted defeat.

Spring cabbages sadly lost their bounce. Irish stew got an import ban.

Pork scratchings were soothed by a lotion, tasting remarkably like ham.

Youngsters with the not-so-young should go to evening classes, to learn

cooking, cleaning, and such, instead of sitting at home on their arses.

Chilli with rice is always nice, not too hot for the average diner. A TV star getting served at the bar remarked:

"I've never tasted anything finer."

Split peas were reunited again; mixed peel went their own separate ways.

Runner beans no longer compete, "it's too expensive to tour these days."

Sour cream was reported for not smiling, and baked beans stayed too long in the sun.

Oranges changed colour last Friday. A black pudding ran off with a nun.

Battered fish eventually recovered from such a terrible ordeal.

Langoustines and haricot beans shared a plate of chips with an eel.

Two cannibals were eating a clown, one said:

"Does yours taste funny?"

The head chef at Mummery's kitchen

was a drummer and played in a group,

the sticks in his grip did a somersault and flip,

and landed in someone's soup.

An American biker stopped at a rundown diner, miles from any town. He had been driving all night and was starving. Ambling up to the counter, he asked the scruffy Latino server,

"Hey, bro, do you have frog-legs?"
The unshaven guy smiled and replied,
"Yeah, we do."
The biker wiped sweat from his face and said,
"Well, hop over the counter, I'll have a double cheeseburger with fries."

Does margarine feel inferior when travelling... because butterflies?

Insanity is heredity... you get it from your children. (Sam Leverson)

Happiness is having a large, loving, close-knit, caring family in another city. (G. Burns)

A boy stood on a burning deck eating cheese and crackers.
A ten-foot flame shot up his frame and burnt the poor sods' knackers.

Bigamy is having one wife too many. Monogamy is the same. (Oscar Wilde)

Identical twins joined the Army and had colleagues and tutors in fits.
Alike in physical structure, Dorothy was the one with tits.

Mothballs are exceptionally well-attended, with no trouble from drunks.

Pigs in blankets have been issued with sleeping bags.

What takes a lot of beating... a wet carpet.

Slow worms have been warned,

"Stop wasting too much frigging' time."

A buxom, middle-aged lady named Sheila

owned a successful souvenir shop,

was once the most popular of persons,

beach streaking without wearing her top.

Cornflour has finally been proved to be no good whatsoever for feet treatment.

Older broad beans were advised to go on diets.

What goes up a chimney down and down a chimney up? A chimney sweep brush. (A rare sight nowadays)

Wild rhubarb was notified to...

"CALM THE F..K DOWN."

Hummingbirds have been given free lessons on how to whistle.

I have never seen one eating fish or sipping a fine, rich claret.

Or water-skiing on a lake, what can it be? A parrot.

Quite a few nonsense compositions were created during a depression period, but the unusual verse has nothing to do with the Prozac-based pills. I don't need mind-altering stimulus to create; you should see my paintings if you want something to talk about! I sent a sample of my artwork to a well-known children's book illustrator/editor. He admired my work but could not actively advise where it might be used and wished me well. Another editor on a nameless website suggested I attend group therapy and mind-awareness sessions.

I did not understand what he meant. Aren't people odd? You cannot please them all, can you?

One simple autograph-signed verse was written by my wife's mother in the nineteen-thirties (Katherine Mary Cook), which reads...

"My heart is like a cabbage, when 'tis split in two, the leaves I give to many, but my heart I give to you." (1940's)

Marriage is a partnership where, no matter how good a husband is, his wife is still the better half.

What range of mountains sounds like a body part? Pair-a-knee's (Pyrenees).

This has nothing to do with The Owl and the Pussycat.

The trowel and a dozy twat hired a canoe and went upstream.

Both wore warm woolly hats, coloured a delicate shade of green.

"What are we looking for?" asked a trowel to the dozy twat.

"Not sure, old mate. Look everywhere, a large parcel, something like that."

Last Tuesday, I looked up an old friend... what a ghastly sight.

Pea's pudding hot, pea's pudding cold

Pea's pudding in the pot, nine days old.

Ghosts in the Afternoon

For a welcome change this afternoon,

ghosts visited and chatted

there were no formal introductions

pleasantries never mattered

Old friends and colleagues smiled and laughed,

talked about where they'd been

Some had changed where some had not.

It was a friendly, sociable scene.

I was surprised at forthright attitudes,

where once reluctant speech was shown,

Eyes sparkled, strong handshakes given,

secrets told, confidence had grown.

Greeting kisses came from lips

long ago contemplative questioning,

anecdotes and mundane topics

were somehow not worth mentioning.

Shrill female laughter pierced the air.

Girlfriends hugged and cried.

conversations were openly discussed

where before were only implied.

Chefs and police officers, lawyers, wheeler-dealers

An apprentice estate agent was putting out feelers.

All chatted about life, food and the weather,

someone fell over a large flowerpot, young big bosomy clerk Heather.

A mail carrier at the door disturbed the scene, ghost visitors all disappeared.

A vague lavender scent remained, my headache suddenly cleared.

Alibis and bare-faced lies were in a competition,

against a loud crowd without a single ambition.

Leading was "Sorry I'm late." Second "I missed my bus."

Way back in third place "I've fallen over, please don't make a fuss."

Coming up from behind them "couldn't find my shirts" closely followed "I overslept"

then "my arm aches, it bloody hurts."

"I completely forgot" was out of breath, lagging too was "I'm on a diet."

An enormous wobbly in a too-small leotard puffed…

"I'm being sponsored, so have to try it."

'I've got the wrong trainers on,' a skinny voice replied

she fell over a yoga mat and cried and cried and cried.

An educated young miss from Brighton did charity work for a laugh.

Painted her body red, did cartwheels on her bed, wearing only a smile and a scarf.

A re-trained ogre named Derek with the strength of a working horse,

was successfully given treatment for dunking hamsters in raspberry sauce.

His teeth were like a lighthouse. When he smiled, they beamed.

When he played football, it was an earthquake taking place,

if taking a free kick, the football disappeared into space.

Magliski's Hotel has a ghost with no head,

it's in room number nine, at the foot of a bed.

Pin-striped Periwinkles never like to dine

'Cos they easily get pissed up drinking cheap red Spanish wine.

Sparkling hedgehogs wearing tiaras and crowns,

swore at the acrobats and were rude to the clowns.

Margarita Manthorpe, dancing with the mayor,

began taking all her clothes off, she didn't really care.

Down to bra and G-string suddenly announced,

"I'm an hour late for my Pilates" and out the door, she flounced.

Twisted yellow Tremlees went into a trance.

While Philamenia Straken began cycling to France.

Gargantuan noisy pigeons dived from high-rise houses.

Broke into shops and stole dresses, hats and trousers.

Two kangaroos boxing near Hammersmith Bridge,

one accused the other of pinching food from their 'fridge.

Three whistling caterpillars and a yodelling boa snake

auditioned for TV but never got a break.

A young woman wearing only a smile

mounted a choirboy and stopped rehearsals for a while.

A glass-blowing grasshopper wore an old T-shirt and jeans

while a crying baby crocodile sat in a bath full of baked beans.

Tap-dancing mushrooms fell off a sink,
just as Larry the lugworm wanted a drink.

Gabbery Gimlets chewing on ants,
destroyed garden furniture and weed down their pants.

Voluminous venomous treacherous scats

were invited to London but had to wear hats.

Rare Galapoochy humming crows had flown away to God only knows,

before they left, leaving a note

"Please keep the expensive plants afloat."

Wrestling sheep were winning their bout

when a farmer turned up and kicked them all out.

A rainbow danced with a scarecrow, one afternoon quite late

they pranced, laughed and yelled aloud then jumped a tall metal gate.

A black and white cow saw them, asked "Can I have a dance?"

Rainbow said he didn't mind. Scarecrow muttered "You got one chance."

The three new friends met a limping crow, his feathers misshapen and bent.

Rainbow asked, "Is it painful like that?" Crow answered, "I live in a tent."

The four of them met a squirrel who wore red-coloured Wellington boots.

They saw an owl and inquired how he was. "I really don't give two hoots."

The five of them went into a shop to order a nice pot of tea

but white mice serving customers announced, "We close at half-past three."

"Why are you always playing with your balls?"
"Nobody else will do it."

"You said your dog has no nose,

how does he smell, bloody awful?"

When is a door not a door? When it's ajar.

I put good money on a horse for the 2.30. It came in at 4.45.

One more drink and I would have been under the host (Dorothy Parker).

"That dog ate all the Bourbons," "That takes the biscuit."

The Egg Cups

Two conjoined egg cups Sid and Eric had a day out in town instead of being shut away in a kitchen cupboard. The weather was fine and sunny. Lots of people shopping and walking in streets. Standing beside a fruit and vegetable stall in the marketplace, a bunch of grapes asked if the egg cups would give them a lift.

"Of course," smiled Eric, and they carried the grapes to a baker's shop.

Seeing what the grapes had done, two smart lemons shouted out, "Can we get a lift?"

"Of course," grinned Sid to Eric and took the lemons to a butcher.

When they reached their next destination, the lemons pointed to mates coming towards them.

Two juicy pears waved. "Got room for us, please?" Both lemons agreed. "Course we have."

Watching nearby, two huge oranges winked at one another and began to say, "Can you take us to," but the egg cups were off!

They hurried back to the house, jumped up into the kitchen cupboard and looked forward to carrying ONLY EGGS.

A large, black-faced rabbit with a wheelbarrow sat on a log near a road.

He was out of breath and resting because of a heavy load.

A farmer asked, "Can you deliver straw to my manager's wife, Mrs Day?"

The gasping rabbit didn't know the fact that the lady lived five miles away.

I wrote two brief letters to dear Spike Milligan, bless him. I loved the crazy poetry, nutty books and general outlook on life and his hardships.

A cassette which he narrates is one of my many favourite pieces of music. Called *Snow Goose*, it is based on a real-life character. It is heart-warming and sad when a hunchback artist recluse who cared for birds and small animals, somewhere desolate in the Essex marshlands, falls in love with a young girl (Fritha) who brought him an injured goose. The atmospheric background music helps set scenes of a year of recovery, which was during D-Day in WW2.

Spike was an individual character among celebrities, and attending a presentation including the then Prince Charles, only Spike would get away with what he said with a wide grin (about Prince Charles): "Snivelling little bastard." The audience burst into uncontrolled laughter. Such was the magnetism Spike created.

On the reverse side of the cassette, the group CAMEL gave an interpretation of the same subject. Expert musicians follow the goose's antics with detail and complicated rhythms, with true finesse.

The second time of writing, I enclosed a couple of my encaustic wax paintings. He thanked me for the kind gesture and mentioned he hadn't been well but was busy writing his next book.

I treasure those two replies, which are kept in the same envelope as Sir George Martin's answer to a comment I made about his production of *In My Life*. Beatles tunes sung by celebrities: Billy Connolly, Jim Carrey, Goldie Hawn, John Williams, Celine Dion and others. Wonderfully different renditions.

The distinctive tonal voice of Sean Connery narrates the title of the CD and is one of the most emotional renditions of someone else's record.

He (Sir George) explained my letter had gone astray when his overseas recording studio survived a tornado. He kindly signed a photograph, which I will keep for posterity.

The original version of *In My Life* by the Beatles was a beat ballad, whereas Sean Connery's narrative is a world away, with stronger sentiment that pierces the conscience of former friendships, brings a lump to the throat or tears from once-loved special involvements.

Having musical interests, I always listen to lyrics that 'say something' before giving my opinion of the music in totality. Words are easy when composing a song, but session musicians and music directors are the miracle workers. They create masterpieces from scribbled notes on scraps of paper.

With current electronics, gizmos, and unimagined ingenuity, an orchestra with choir, strings, and full accompaniment can be produced from a single keyboard.

I never owned a complete drum kit. Made do with well-used, cheap and cheerful oddments, nothing expensive or showy, but adequate for getting people on their feet and dancing to what I was playing. Great! One item of interest I was given was a loose-head pigskin African drum that could be played by hand and produced a deep tone and was usually hung from a nearby chair. My minuscule Olympic claret red "outfit" was a 14 x 6 snare, 18 x 10 bass drum partly padded. Hi-hat foot assembly (awful unmatched thick cymbals) and one other cymbal, which I drilled and added paperclips to use as a sizzle. Would have been overawed to have sat behind today's top drummers' set-ups with too many cymbals, electronic effects, control panel and double bass drums. Too much energy required! Have never played properly "miked up." Must be great.

In My Life

There are places I'll remember all my life,

though some have changed some forever, not the better

Some have gone and some remain. All these places had their moments, with lovers and

friends, I can still recall,

some are dead and some are living. In my life, I've loved them all.

But of all these friends and lovers, there is no one compared with you,

and these mem'ries lose their meanings

when I think of love as something new.

Though I'll never lose affection for people and things that went before

I know I'll often stop and think about them,

In my life I'll love you more, in my life I'll love you more.

Occasionally, when we have guests, my wife and I offer a repartee on poems or expressions we know. Not every attentive face appreciates our effort, but we don't mind. Are we eccentric? Perhaps! I feel fine.

One rendition is Spike's short piece which goes, "I must go down to the sea again to the rolling sea and sky. I left my vest and pants there. I wonder if they are dry?"

'I'm not so think and as you drunk I am.' (John Squire)

A few paragraphs on RAF incidents to give a sample on what went on having left trade training (it was called "passing out") into Man Service. My first posting was Marham in Norfolk, on the Kings Lynn to Norwich Road. I was the youngest cook, so became known as junior. Fair enough.

To those intelligent readers that know what desserts are (sweets to others) I relive the following incident, which was one of the first jobs on a night shift, aged seventeen, as a SAC (senior aircraftsman).

No doubt some of you have not heard of blancmange (blahmonge) as its popularity has disappeared over the years the same as sago, semolina and tapioca. Have enjoyed the unique flavours of each product. Lovely grub, a wash and a scrub. Most folk sneer their noses at such a declaration.

From school of trade training where you catered for six persons, now thrust into an enormous commercial-size kitchen with lofty ceilings, powerful over-head fans constantly whirred to agitate and remove cooking smells and intense heat from heavy, black-faced cast-iron doors, diesel-fired, deep cavern-like ovens. Large steam-fed boilers glinted from massive fluorescent high-up tubed lighting. A piercing annoying wall telephone constantly intruded into my work schedule, although I had an older aide for help if I required any.

It was quicker to do it myself! He was a TAG (trade assistant general) a kind of 'go-for' and could work in the motor vehicle yard, helping washing-up, a general help. None-the-less, he could make good coffee, at least had one thing going for him.

Totally alone after cooking and serving squadron meals, RAF police ordering coffee and sandwiches for security bods, as well as off-duty staff members traipsing-in for a free meal before bed; I felt like a flea on a pig's back, new to a demanding strenuous never-ending regime of bulk catering management.

After locking the front and rear doors of the mess, turning steam feeds off, shutting many high-up windows and slowing-down ceiling fans, silence enveloped yours truly, but it was never feet-up in catering. The entire kitchen area, which included servery, plate wash, rear corridor, staff rest room and toilets and a walk-in fridge room, all were swept then lightly mopped over, which must have taken at least one hour. Never timed it. After that, all lighting in the dining rooms (up and downstairs) were turned off with only the central boiler area lit up. Checked that all large and small boilers were empty and cleaned and ready for the next day's usage. One careless duty-cook (not me) had forgotten there were at least twenty chickens in one boiler, ready for curry BUT had not mentioned this to the nightshift cook. By the morning, there was a dreadful stink to greet the early shift workers.

Having the lid closed with no circulating air caused the submerged and floating cluck-clucks to 'go-ff.' Nothing could be done but went straight into the garbage bins in the rear yard. I never knew what happened because I was on my three days off. Things like that were rare but would not like to have been in the shoes of the duty cook. That is why there were many things to consider whenever on your own during nights. It was a responsible aspect all cooks had a reliable memory and an excellent sense of smell. I must have saved thousands of pounds' worth of meat, bread, vegetables, and pastries over the years, and I am still proud of that ownership!

Blowing my ego trumpet, I could over-ride oven clocks by a few minutes and call out to members on my shift... "Whose doing roast meats?" Or "pastries are ready."

And welcomed praise when magnificent Yorkshire puddings were unloaded from the long black oven trays: like tiny mountain ranges, brown and crisp!

I prepared next day's sweet course, which consisted of dozens of fruit pies, rice pudding, multiple crumbles, plus the dreaded blancmange. Rolling-out pastries large scale was physically tiring. Chest and shoulder muscles ached, fulfilling the repetitive exertions required.

It was bewildering to an apprehensive young chap about to add water into a deep fish kettle (heavyweight metal container) and a sweet-smelling small dune of pink powder. Slowly turned the hot-water boiler tap on to allow a controllable flow of water into the aromatic powder, while stirring with a king-size whisk. BUT THEN, a rapidly setting mixture develops, which thickened by the second. Oh, buggering angels. Something was wrong and hurriedly turned off the tap to peer into the almost solid mass, then realise. Should have added COLD WATER into the cement-like enormity, gradually adding diluted Carnation tinned milk. Many tins were used!

That's the way we learned by stupid silly mistakes, then hopefully we don't do it the second time. Looking back to those ex-trainee experiences was an utterly new world of multi-tasking even before the word was invented. We did it yonks ago, oh yes, we did.

I recall a Jimmy Simpson, an elderly rotund corporal who joined up as an Air Gunner/cook who surprisingly thickened soups with porridge.

He was much older than us. At the mention of Jimmy's name, all staff would immediately smile because of his remarkable likeness to the cartoon character Mr Magoo. I can see him now. His cooking methods were not from any recipe book or manual, and how he attained his rank was a mystery. He was a danger to himself because the shoes he wore in the hectic, crowded mess kitchen were more like slippers, silly old bugger. But he was a character and seemed to have a good relationship with staff and personnel on the other side of the counters. I think he must have met His Master Chef many moons ago. He was a Geordie. Had a slight difficulty with loose-fitting dentures when the bottom set might suddenly appear when getting refills from the low deep cupboards under the serving counters. Good old Jimmy, what a guy?

Another character, also a Geordie, was a valet in the officers' mess and always had jokes to tell, between entering and disappearing through swing doors into the dining room. Came from Wallsend, once a monumental ship-building city. He was going to train as a welder but witnessed a mate of his get terrible burns from an accident, so the idea was cancelled; then RAF-bound, he signed on for the least time and when trade names changed, he became a steward. Loved his native brew, and I saw results of over-indulgence more than once, from night-time drinking at either or both popular pubs in Swaffham. Rose and Crown or the Greyhound. Bluddy grate mon.

Personally, I never felt home sick at all. Yes, it was strange living with twenty similarly aged youths from all corners of Britain. Hearing Scottish dialects was one more new thing to young, innocent ears. Learnt swear words in record time and was surprised when a few older lads were allowed to smoke!

Paddy Moore came from Drogheda in southern Ireland and never wore his uniform when on leave; he would have been shot apparently if seen in RAF blue. Several newcomers were ex-ATC (air training corps) and knew service rules and regulations; some had flown gliders.

One chap had been a nurse, while quite a few worked on the land or in chicken factories. One Norfolk bod was an assistant to a manager that ran a piggery. An Essex lad was a telegram boy riding a small BSA motor bike. It was amazing looking back, how quickly every entrant got to know each other and became friends. Very amiable indeed. It was easy to break the ice between total strangers.

We trained together on the parade ground for marching drills and handling an ancient 303 rifle which was used during World War 2. Within practical cookery classes we did our initial lessons to absorb reams of recipes, diagrams and written work pertaining to catering. Even had to study the digestive system. Notebooks were filled with extra facts on nourishment, dietary control, a new method of cooking called microwave, and hygiene. It was never-ending but essential to thoroughly get acquainted with the comprehensive information.

My first choice to learn a trade in the RAF was driver/mechanic but I was appointed my second choice: catering. Much later it was explained my maths paper had let me down. There were lots of figures and formulae within mechanics, which wouldn't have helped me!

Besides factors associated with a historic background of service life, I saw films about the First World War, transport documentaries, a brief sex instruction on venereal disease, and continued scholastic pursuits that were needed for exams.

Admittedly, while watching films, there were times we could nod off, apart from an observant corporal drill instructor giving sleeping lads a flick around the ears from a newspaper he kept for that purpose.

A loud banging on the front door of the billet announced a drill instructor (DI) entering, who would instruct "bulling up" boots we had worn that day. To absolute beginners of this fundamental necessity, it was torture to the index finger, which would be encased in a bright yellow soft rag with Kiwi black shoe polish applied and for the next two hours, you gently rubbed the sticky polish in small circles into the black leather footwear. Continuously offering a dab into a saucer of cold water until dimples of the new boots were not visible. Every entrant sat on the edge of his bed or at a table, if you had one, repeating this procedure until a shine slowly appeared from perpetual finger-twirling. Shame that nobody thought about filming this vital but tedious task for posterity. Clothing caused problems when wearing new crisp underwear, attached collars and tight boots for day-to-day use. Rashes around the neck from the starch content, cellular drawers (pants) promoted constant itching down the crotch area, and blisters quickly made an appearance from the heavy studded boots. And the blessed beret. This had to be placed in cold water and manually pulled, pushed and wrung out to allow a correct fitting. The second attendance of RAF exchanged clothing stores resembled scenes from the *Carry On* film series but featured half-dressed immature young men instead of glamorous celebrities and film stars.

Staff doing the issuing cast brief glances towards each recruit, spun round on their heels into a curtained door entrance and selected whatever was required, whether working blue trousers and tunic, SD (service dress) shiny peak caps for parades and station functions, greatcoats, or PT kit. It was organised chaos until everybody was booted and suited to the best ability and told to "fall in outside and SHUT UP" by the drill instructor, who craftily had a quick smoke behind an outside toilet block. Heavens, those clothes were so uncomfortable against teenage skin. Eight lads developed the "dreaded pubic itch", for which treatment was a grey-coloured salve resembling butter but wonderfully curative. Nothing could be done about blisters, although NAAFI sales of plasters and powders skyrocketed.

Being married to a serviceman was not an ideal situation for many women. The fact being, every two to three years at one camp, there would be another upheaval and stress of being posted to anywhere throughout the world, which was not welcomed by couples. It was hard at first making friends, acclimatising yourself to new surroundings, settling in and then having to "up sticks" and go somewhere else.

I recall getting a pre-posting notification to the remote Kingdom of Saudi Arabia (Aden) and suffered an asthma attack from the shock. I notified the addressees and got the posting deferred, only to be informed two months later I was to go to a North Africa posting in Libya, which was fifteen miles into a desert. El Adem had been an Italian airfield before becoming British-run and part of WW2 defences, with association to Tobruk, vital in several battles.

Led by German General Rommel, it was a terrible loss for British Eighth Army personnel who had to surrender to a superior task force. He made an astonishing statement by saying, "Give me the British Army and I will conquer the world."

I lived in Tobruk, a crumbling ex-war-torn town, where Arabs lived in bombed-out buildings and attempted to exist as best they could in dire surroundings. It was unreal to see severely damaged run-down structures being inhabited by families with babies, wild Pi-dogs, chickens and hard-worked mules and donkeys, in the noisy dust-blown area near Church Square and surrounding unmade streets. It was quite a visual shock when first seen!

Twenty years later it became a vital deep-water base and the world's fifth oil-producing country. It is now a fabulously progressive city with magnificent Byzantine, Roman and Turkish artefacts, historic underwater towns, and ultra-modern highways. Some walkways (then) were non-tarred, but shingle for basic underfoot surfaces. It was hellish when it rained.

For forty Libyan pounds per month (furniture was hired) from nineteen sixty-five until nineteen sixty-seven, life in a hot climate where camels proudly ambled in from their nomadic desert encampments and sandstorms threatened breathing during a squall; life for a twenty-two-year-old guy could not have been more memorable, impressionable and a beautiful experience. I would love to travel back to Libya and see the difference it is today. Much has been done since our once-in-a-lifetime two-year posting. It will be within my heart and socks forever!

Other places visited were Derna, Cyrene, Apollonia, Benghazi, and Bardia. I could add more travel ventures but must control my meanderings. It was truly unforgettable.

We attempted the Arabic idiom, which shopkeepers appreciated with wide smoke-stained toothy smiles and handshakes. Attending the same coffee shop, it was cleaner, brighter, with a granite chequered floor (compared to others in town). The larger-than-life overweight Egyptian man spoke perfect English, having studied in Oxford. He was instantly fascinated by my eldest daughter's blonde hair, which had turned white by the sun. Arabs are enormously family-orientated, and we were given edible gifts when we left for England. All Arabs have black hair!

It was far from television news nowadays and will be a cherished memory for as long as I live. It was the most fascinating of all postings. I left a bit of my heart there!

Arriving from the UK, we were informed (warned) about delightful little blood-sucking crawlies called bedbugs, not to be mistaken for cockroaches. Both pests were horrid and a damned irritant. The latter could be found in masses, including an outside bin compound where wet swill, meal scraps, vegetables and disused oil from fryers were parked before local certified collectors took them away in battered ex-Army lorries.

At night-time you could hear the buggers scurrying across the corrugated roofing of the patio patch where all sorts of rubbish and crap were untidily discarded. Rats were everywhere, bloody horrible nose-twitching, ever-jumping grot-box vermin. They grew huge, fat and scary. Nobody liked them. They existed uncontrolled but a nonchalant attitude was normal.

There was no deterrent plan. Somebody was told the locals ate rats as a readily available meat source.

We must have used gallons of a green disinfectant fluid to rid the creatures from climbing up and into partly opened metal lids of bins, which should have been forcibly closed.

It made shivers go down the spine when dozens of them moved as one to another corner of the backyard enclosure.

Other traders said, "Cooks had it easy," to which I readily respond, "BOLLOCKS." We were on the go more than other tradespeople and women. Health and safety standards were non-existent in those bygone times. It was miraculous that we did not go down with an illness or disease.

Beneath each bed leg we added three inches of a foul-smelling ghastly liquid to prevent both problem visitors attempting to elevate themselves to the sleeping, sweating nude bodies in the two-tier bunk beds. Before getting acclimatised to night heat, when awakening, where you had lain was the outline wet shape of your body. It was awful at first, but apart from going outside to sleep on concrete slabs of the pavements, we survived. Luckily, there was never any bother by mosquitoes; that would have been tough shit (as they say). Good job for the jabs we had!

Army bods doing "desert warfare training" would be utilised in RAF kitchens, more a punishment than part of cooking routines, with petty annoyances popping up now and again. The Middlesex Regiment contained lads that had their heads shaved, not the thing to do where the temperature exceeded ninety degrees. Nutters.

For this act of "self-abuse" they were charged and appointed to do chores within our mess hall. Quite a lot of Army bods couldn't give a toss and had odd ideas on creating nuisances of themselves. This did not go down well with the warrant officer in charge of messing and, in fact, banned the Army from working anywhere near the kitchen. Which was fine by the cooks.

One lad we had was charged for an offence of "misuse of RAF equipment" and related what he had done... we burst out laughing.

He put his brand-new issue boots into a boiler daily used for making custard. Asking why he had done such a silly thing, he simply responded, "We do it all the time, the heat assists shaping the leather for a better fitting." What can you say? All Army bods did the same thing.

One grossly offensive and cruel after-tea pursuit was to try to find spiders and beetles and, on occasions, a unique creature, a chameleon, that would dangle precariously from under one of the few bushes on the sand and gravel grounds bordering the accommodation buildings. It might appear comical, but the intent was serious as part of entertainment to pass off-duty hours.

These men were on their own and ANYTHING was open to be chosen as amusement. It was funny with men half stripped off, glistening from head to toe from sun-tan oils, some wore silly floppy hats or self-made head coverings, bending down, crouching, armed with bits of wood or stick, peering beneath small boulders or shaking the sparse greenery of bushes, anticipating falling wildlife from hidden places, it was funny.

When or if a mislodged bug, fly, or grotesque, horrible camel spider came into view, many screams and childish yells caused onlookers (there were always onlookers) to join in with handclapping, whistling and calling out with earnest applications of rude words, which went unheard.

Normal after-tea-time plans were to sit on the steps leading from the block, with cups of steaming-hot sweet tea, and swat as many as possible of the ever-swarming, intruding, bloody fruit flies that hovered, laughing at the humans below. Lighter fuel fumes wafted across the open ground as the poor undefended ants, and other scurrying escaping things, were instantly burnt and shrivelled. All gone and forgotten in a few crazy seconds.

Such was the routine everyone owned a plastic fly swat. DIY nerds made their own and they were heavier than bought ones. We assumed the smell of sun-tan oil caused two to three squadrons of the moronic, menacing flies to dive headlong towards bodies and bite any white flesh with their proboscis weapons. It made you itch simply glancing at them. Tiny flitting bloodsuckers.

Camel spiders were like a science fiction creature. They could grow to table-plate size and gave a serious bite if you got that close. If you hit one with a flip-flop, it would shrug its hairy body, stretch feathery crawly legs, lie closer to the ground and, walking away, grow back to its original size and could outrun the average service member. UGH.

By the time I finished my fifteen-year career, a new meals system was to become an everyday practice, which was BRUNCH, breakfast until lunchtime.

Not the only new introduction was the scheme to pre-order the next day's meal. I was not involved, so do not know how it was accepted, but would suspect it was to do with food wastage. I could be wrong!

There was an exceptional amount of food wastage from every meal, lunches especially. No wonder farmers were eager to collect swill. There was money to be made in leftovers. You would not believe how many large heavy bins were full to overflowing every week. Items not allowed were tea leaves, coffee grounds and rhubarb leaves. Gives animals the shits.

Steam-fed food serving counters no longer exist. We stood and served customers as they slowly passed. Sounds extremely old-fashioned, but it worked for decades throughout every RAF station!

Massive walk-in steamers created trays of Eartha Kitt legs (chocolate sponge puddings in cylindrical sleeves), which brought smiles on faces, mainly because a delicious chocolate sauce accompanied each serving. Far too much sugar content, but deliciously satisfying.

There are no longer preparation instructions written in chalk on a blackboard. Amen to that. Examples should have been saved for reference, to see how varied a menu was and the choices, all those years ago.

I would have liked to visit "modern" stations to see how far we have come since those physically hard-worked shifts when cooks sweated their bollocks off in unimaginable heat and multi-tasked all the time. It was hard graft and anyone thinking catering for the masses was easy was always welcome to commit themselves to a mid-week morning shift.

Returning briefly to my motorcycling experiences, I send my most sincere apologies to a young man that wanted a lift from Downham Market to camp. His name was Doug Haliburton, who left the pub with a full set of functioning fingers but, by the time we got back to his billet, had a disfigured little finger. Because of mud on the twisty, mud-spattered road, I skidded sideways towards a gate leading into a field. The mud was from nearby tractors.

Doug fell off before I let go. The bike came to a halt, inches before colliding against the metal gate. Running up the road to get the bike without seeing how my passenger was, I picked up the machine and walked back with it. Matey sat on the grass edge looking at his bent pinkie. I wonder if he ever had it straightened. We were able to finish getting back to camp.

The bike was fine and the last time I saw Doug he smiled and said, "You have given me a souvenir from a free lift. Can't be bad?"

This was the first effort at writing poetry, dated 1986.

"That's All."

Goodbye my love, please no tears, don't make me feel this bad.

Our last cheerio, our sad farewell it makes me feel so sad.

This journey ahead without you. I hate to end like this.

a fond goodbye, a lump in the throat, come close, one last kiss.

I will never ever forget you, your smile, soft hands, your voice.

No consolation in my heart, one day perhaps, rejoice

Adieu, my sweet, bon voyage may all your troubles be small.

suffering will eventually vacate, my heart will break, that's all.

I am not a foodie in the genuine sense, keep an eye on my weight and look for new products in shops and am ably experienced turning my hand to anything food-wise but attempting to make a pig's ear into a silk purse eluded my expertise.

As a personal comment towards everyday eating, I need to express my distaste and loathing concerning controversial continental cuisine. Once upon a time, these two obscene meals were popular. I cannot believe that a family would sit down and feast upon these repulsive ingredients, namely, Toad-in-the-hole and Bird's Nest Soup. Whosoever invented such sickening dishes should be horse-whipped, kicked over the nearest wall and tossed into the North Sea without a life jacket.

The first challenge is to get the slithery, fidgety wet-skinned creatures into a deep hot pan containing Yorkshire pudding batter, mixed vegetables chopped with herbs and to prevent their energetic flailing, swimming legs splattering everywhere. Toads have terrific strength and are well known to hop great distances from being caught. They also screech aloud as the heat gets too much for them. Horrendous.

Above all this, the technique when serving leaves a lot to be desired because they are likely to explode as a sharp knife penetrates the skin as it is lowered into the roasting pan. The alarming noise is equally off-putting to others chomping at their chosen meal. That's why they are no longer on menus? To those admiring this delicacy, good luck to your stomachs and hope you have enough pills and powders to eliminate feelings of nausea, uncontrollable flatulence, and severe cramps.

It is also unfair to other eaters in the dining room.

Not the same, but similar, is when Bird's Nest Soup was featured. To lucky customers with a full set of pure-white, mortgage-paid toothy-pegs, there is no worry, but to most chopper-owners, moments when tiny twigs get stuck between fillings can cause coughing, hiccups, or serious choking. Can be scary, even dangerous.

Be alert, you are spending good money on first-class professional cooking.

Ask if the nests have been par-boiled overnight, marinated with spices and herbs. You might be alarmed at the answer. Dubious takeaways do not bother and scald them before sautéing but it doesn't give the same delicate taste. Regular eatery critics spot too many shortcuts. Any underhanded aspects of food, hygiene and presentation should be reported immediately, not a week later, having tea and a bun with Aunt Grace at the new trendy Munch Mob bistro. Complain at once!

Not too long ago, a feature in a posh catering magazine brought interest in dodgy goings-on within culinary outlets. Chicken's feet casserole/stew. It was a double-page, fully coloured agency report conducted by trainee (Chinese) college staff. They discovered a practice of adding goose and duck feet with small birds' appendages to bulk up the content, which did not go down well with the Far Eastern communities. It is not enjoyable when diners do not know where they (the feet) had been. Treading grapes for wine, crushing apples for cider, or squelching and skidding in riverside mud. It is appalling to think such underhanded intentional methods are going on in today's "modern caring, educated world." I am lost for words. It certainly takes many people to do all sorts of idiotic and deplorable acts of dishonesty, even within a commercial outlet as catering. It is not right. Unsavoury. Distasteful.

What is the difference between a baby's sore bum and a locomotive train? Both have tender behinds.

Her teeth were like stars. they came out at night.

Sixty-six tall twin smart smiling Siamese sisters shouted, sitting in saunas sipping sweet aperitifs, while young boys smiled and played with themselves.

You should know the original "Hey Diddle Diddle the Cat and the Fiddle." Straw piddle piddle the prat wanted a widdle, the sow was proud of plants she had grown. A small dog fainted, his kennel someone painted, and a sole was left on its own.

Horses and carts with wees and farts are delightful to watch as they pass, passengers not aware stand and stare, while the driver sees only an arse.

An American lady from Boulder won a beauty show when she was older, dancing the tango while eating a mango, lifted her breasts over her shoulder.

Going back to music. Worth mentioning our local theatre throughout the years has seen wonderful acts which were tremendous. Georgie Fame, Alan Price, Danny La Rue, Joe Brown, George Melly, Bernie Clifton. A Russian Ballet Company brought a seldom popular genre and it was the first time I saw Swan Lake performed with sedate, elegant displays from accomplished dancers. Saw Val Doonican at The Sparrow's Nest Theatre.

The Grimethorpe Colliery Band received well-earned encores from cheering full-house fans, while the Pasadena Roof Orchestra played music from the 1920s, accordingly attired, with a comical theme running throughout their enjoyable repertoire.

The most memorable show was certainly Ken Dodd and his Diddy Men. He kept us totally in his grasp until one in the morning. Never experienced such continuous laughter and jollity. Jokes were unending and his singing was brilliant. Sang several of his hits including 8 x 10, The River and Love Is Like a Violin. Magic! Has a comforting voice.

Playing at The Theatre Royal in Norwich, The Baker Gurvitz Army was magnificent, featuring Ginger Baker (Cream), the Gurvitz Brothers and Mr Snips singing his heart out. Stage presentation was spot-on. They had quality and were one of the best groups of the time. Ginger created murmuring from the packed audience by stating "Good evening, Ipswich" before commencing the evening, a great way of "audience participation", I thought. It was a terrific show.
Ginger is no longer with us, but his techniques are still being copied!

The only time we encountered an empty venue featured a concert pianist and a tenor at the Marina. I counted the attendees prior to the lights going out, only thirty-three people downstairs... how terrible and embarrassing for the two musicians.

We knew the pianist Robert Rampling because he had visited our home previously via his mum and dad. We went to their home and were shown where he kept his instrument. It was at the bottom of a large, neat garden within an air-conditioned, soundproof brick building. That was the only time we saw him and have not heard or seen him since.

On my own, I was enthralled and satisfied to see the "singer's singer" Jack Jones. I listened, mesmerised, transfixed. It was wonderful.

It was not mentioned at all on TV, but he died aged eighty-six in October 2024. The Peter Green Splinter Group was another superb evening's entertainment but I did not bother to buy a brochure, tight-fisted git. It was extraordinarily surreal watching the genius blues guitarist-singer play his hits of decades ago, thirty feet from where I sat. The superb backing musicians carried the star himself, who was a shadow of his old mastery.

Got the ticket as proof. He died in 2023. I have many of his original music on cassettes.

Mike Read, EastEnders star and stand-up comedian, zipped through his pitch but on ending, said the risqué jokes' content was part and parcel that "put bums on seats", excusing himself by saying that if anything was coarse or objectionable, he hoped nobody was offended. I was not aware of any rudeness. In fact, it was great!

Television news reported the death of Raymond Froggatt. I briefly spoke to him as he was leaving a Cambridgeshire gig, when a rock and roll singer. Later, he became a country and western star. I asked, "What should I do about the challenge?" He simply replied, "Go where your heart goes." But I could not and left the idea smouldering in my mind. Had asked what I should do. Leave the RAF or become a musician.

On a couple of occasions, I was approached by agents seeking contracts for a German "around Europe" tour. I was serving in HM Forces and could not manage what was required.

The first time being asked about joining an agency was in Huntingdon. The four of us (cannot recall names, it was too long ago) had been doing a twenty-minute half-time break for a Lincolnshire band that was shit-hot, bordering on heavy metal. We played pop music, which was straightforward. I was wringing wet, sweat dripping from efforts of drumming, shirt and trousers sticking to me like a second skin. A guy came up to me as I was about to go into the toilet.

He asked whether I could get to London and meet other band members on a weekend trip to Frankfurt, all expenses paid and return on the Monday. Well! It would have been £200 in my pocket.

A similar "What are you doing next weekend?" came from an older gent who was a scout for a management agency with dancers, singers and ex-holiday camp entertainers on their books.

I explained my position. "You play rock and roll, you play great. Swap your current job and earn good money. You've got it, pal. What do you say?"

It was in a small rural village club hut where all sorts of games were played by the youth of the area, most of them turned up to listen to us. Good for them. Not sure if it was Whaplode Drove, something like that!

The stage was three feet above the dance floor. Hardly room (a usual nuisance in country gigs) for the band's gear and my drums. I was always in a corner at the back.

It was not that easy, I started to tell the bloke who was chatting with another youngster.

One must be sensible, especially when you have service commitments. It would be super and exciting, adventurous, a break from normality, but I COULDN'T DO IT. There would be far too much bullshit paperwork for a start. I faced the fact I would be better off where I was. It might have been a dream materialising, but sense overcame temptation. I stayed an airman!

The Hi-Fi 5 played in one of the roughest pubs in Huntingdon, The Lord Protector. It was a debut appearance but booked as a jazz band. Oh dear… I couldn't do complicated technical stuff. I was a rock drummer, basic, self-taught from listening to records. Happy to play to people. Loved drumming.

Anyway, we set up as usual, did a quick sound check, with me sat at the back of the stage, almost shrouded by massive overhead dangling drapes. The audience was brilliant. Youngsters loved the Rolling Stones, and our repertoire had most of their music, lovely job. Getting whoops, cheers, and other excited noises at the end of each tune was exceptionally rewarding, terrific. Very welcome. They liked us! The second half was good as well.

Several teenage girls came up to the stage and asked for their favourite songs. I am sorry, but the names of the band members escape me. The singer was certainly a fan of Mick Jagger, as he did his job superbly up front, sweating profusely and mimicking the physical effort with great efficiency.

It came to 'Everybody Needs Somebody' when the tempo slows down. The bass drum spurs had worked loose. I had to move to my right, to slide forward to get to the drum. The drum seat slowly tilted. In a split second, pandemonium struck. I tried stopping my forward slip, had to stand up for balance, and naturally grabbed for the huge heavy curtains. The band played on but without my backing beat. The kids in the audience shouted, screamed, stamped feet, and clapped hands, they didn't care about the poor old drummer. I prevented the drum from going over the rim of the stage but accidentally brought down the dust-laden heavy curtains, stroll on. Luckily, after a few adjustments to the percussion instruments, we got through OK. The audience loved it (we were later told) and asked if we were playing again. Great stuff. However, we did not get another booking. It was laughable!

Another slightly amusing anecdote comes to mind when I played in a band where the other guys were all Scots. I cannot recall the name of the band but remember Bob Blair, the singer and rhythm, Harry Hill, lead and singer, with Neil Angus on electrified piano accordion, which was quite unusual for that era. It was winter. Yes, we played when snow was on the ground. The venue was smaller compared to other gigs, and we did not play rock music. The event was a birthday party. We were given a list of chosen tunes, ballads and folk with Latin American thrown in. All the bands I played in could do everything, I was glad to say.

We could do slow dance music when I used a pair of Premier rubber-handled telescopic brushes or soft-headed beaters for cymbal work.

It would be ghastly to play an entire evening at the same musical level. That is why being adaptable was THE THING. This recall features Neil's wonderful expertise on an extremely difficult instrument to play, especially in a heated room after being in the boot of a cold car. Notes within the accordion are created by vibrations of thin metal reeds, lots of them. A few songs progressed until 'Puppet on a String', when suddenly a particular note being fingered produced a loud, squeaking, piercing screech, everyone fell about one female screamed, most continued dancing. Bless their Scottish socks. The fragile reeds had to be warm before progressing; nevertheless, it was all done in the best possible taste. We enjoyed it!

I will not mention the time one of my sticks split, playing a fast rock beat. Nor relate how thin wires on a set of brushes spun off into the audience and got stuck in a girl's hair. Or the time my drum seat adjustment worked loose, and I descended six inches rapidly and very uncomfortably. Neither tell anyone I played one gig wearing new leather cowboy boots and had blisters for days. No, I will not bother with them! I remember Bob came from Prestonpans, Harry from Bathgate and Neil from somewhere in Ayrshire.

My cherished wife and I are great followers of "cover bands", which we have enjoyed immensely. They are true to the originals music-wise, although some lead singers bear no resemblance whatsoever to their figurehead. It does not matter if the music content mimics.

So far, we have seen The Kinks, Roy Orbison, Neil Diamond, AC/DC, Tina Turner, T-Rex, Meatloaf. All were stupendous, with audiences singing along (and dancing) to each respective song. It was nice to hear and showed how dedicated fans are to their favourite bands, heroes and heroines, and age has no barrier to being totally engulfed by the atmosphere musicians create.

Special lighting and stage effects built up both presentation and aura, but over-volume indulgence at times was felt from the electronic panel controller. Older ears are extremely sensitive with hearing aids!

Acquired at least fifty years ago, the best slogan I discovered, now pinned to a wall, states the following and is so true (it would be a sensational car sticker), it reads...

"DO NOT ADJUST YOUR MIND THERE IS A FAULT IN REALITY."

On the first day of every month in my earliest years, and people still do it, I am told, was to say "White rabbits, white rabbits, white rabbits" before you spoke to anyone. It would bring good luck. My wife's mother said a similar thing in the late nineteen-forties, when living in London, "Hares and rabbits and foxes' tails."

My mother believed in superstitious sayings since a young girl. It was maddening.

Seeing rooks or crows flying in circles higher than usual meant "It was a sign of gale-force winds." Sometimes, she was spot-on!

If a female gypsy traveller came to the door with tiny posies, lace, or clothes pegs, I had to answer the door and say, "Mum's on the toilet" and give her a few pennies, because if she wasn't given any money, she would put a spell on the house.

She also muddled words. "Mrs White's son married a maisonette" (majorette) and "Look at those beautiful enemas" (anemones).

Grandfather self-invented sayings: "If it rains when the sun is out, it's a monkey's birthday" "Eat your food and your two fists", with a never explained oddity, "That's not the shirt you've got indoors, is it?"

He used snuff, which made him sneeze. To me, as a small kid, he was a big, broad, tall man with hairy arms and bushy eyebrows. I was his height at fifteen years old.

Both grandparents looked after me, and I loved them. Wandering through their large rear allotment was like trekking through a jungle. It was comforting lying on my back looking to the sky between drooping sunflowers and Brussels sprout stalks. Snails and slugs and fast-running beetles or centipedes did not bother me. I laughed when I picked up worms and threw them over the next-door neighbour's fence. I flicked ladybirds and watched them uncurl their little wings and land safely on a branch or lavender bushes. I revisited their home years after both died, but there were no emotions whatsoever. The kitchen you stepped down into, the dark living room and wood panelling leading up the staircase, had been removed and was now a bright, modernised, spotless property, creating a spacious look.

The large workshop shed and a wartime Anderson shelter in the rear garden were replaced by an open grass and shingle layout, and our sixty-year-old thinning Christmas tree was gone. I felt nothing.

Grandfather pickled boiled eggs and drowned them in a deep glass carboy in liquid called isinglass. I never saw any of them being eaten!

I watched him put clickers on shoes that made tap-dance sounds and gazed in wonderment while he assembled different bits of wood into furniture. He was a master of all trades. A gentle, diligent, adored man.

Grandmother was a person I hardly saw sit still; she was forever flitting about, washing, ironing (she had an electric cable running from a light bulb fitting into the iron), sewing and darning, cooking, and never stood still. I loved them. Both are buried in St Faith's Cemetery, Norwich. RIP my wonderful grandparents. I still miss them very much!

Their house was in Commodore Road, facing Caldecott Road, from where I fished on the roadway path. On the grass opposite was a raised verge where I train-spotted. Nothing has changed since those faraway happy times, except that the road over-floods.

Youngsters and older fishing fans still cast out their lines from the same length of pathway I did, all those innocent, young, adventurous years ago!

Within an enormous transparent bubble throbs not a million unaccomplished ambitions. One harsh, threatening, wrong word could pierce the delicate membrane and destroy a lifetime's aim to be known for both my creativity in artwork and literary content.

I sleep through numerous dreams but never know their origin. Water portrays dangerous images, yet I have dived into clear, deep water from high-up structures lots of times. Can fly. All I do is step out with longer strides, then slowly ascend and enjoy being like a bird. I am not scared. Do not fly too high or too far because I need to get back (to where?). A 'mind doctor' could interpret these repetitive occurrences? Sitting on a toilet WC seat, I have been talking to customers sat at tables having a meal is one such silly dream. And walking naked in numerous situations is another. Driving an exceptionally tall bus, I manoeuvre through narrow streets without hitting anything. I can saw through wood and metal using my hands; there is no blood, and it does not hurt. Whenever there is a sign of violence and I attempt to hit my aggressor, my fist goes through their body?

I am driving a car which alters into a bicycle before changing into another form of transport but never feel anything through my hands, and there is always a fault with a handbrake; must constantly pull the lever upwards until I feel it engage but still does not work properly. That happens often!!!??

Imagine two Scotsmen from any large city (strong accents, yer ken?) jokingly talking sarcastically to a non-Scottish person.

One Scot says to the English guy, "So, you consider you can talk our tongue, do you? Well, quickly repeat this three times in your best dialect, OK?"

The Englishman agrees, clears his throat, swallows and takes a deep breath, then says, "I canna hold a hot totty in mah hond. I canna hold a hot totty in mah hond. I canna hold a hot totty in mah hond."

Both Scots face the Englishman and say, "WELL, STICK IT UP YER AIRSE." (Which was hilariously funny the first time I heard it.)

I lived in the Highlands of Scotland, Alness in Ross-shire, for two years, halfway up a mountain in a caravan, with a baby, during the worst weather in a long time. My eldest daughter was born in Raigmore Hospital, Inverness.

The only source of heating came from a tiny open fire near the door of the Astral Advance, bought from North Vans of Wick, close to John O' Groats. I could not find proper accommodation in town, and we could move the caravan if I got another posting. Our body heat and the pathetic warmth from the fire caused condensation to run down the aluminium walls freely. It was unhygienic with an incredibly young baby. Our bed was a seat by day, and a handle thing enabled it to be lowered onto the floor.... Bob's yer firkin uncle, it turned into a comfortable double bed.

Nappies were soaked and boiled in a bucket on top of a small gas cooker. It was no joke. It did us well until I was posted again, but it sure was crazy.

When the weather was perfect and sunny with a hint of a breeze, we would take crisps, chocolate and fruit (if we remembered) and do something not even locals bothered with. We set off to climb a steep, shrub-covered, boulder-strewn mini-mountain named Fyrish. Approaching the highest ground, the view was terrific; you could see for miles. On our left-hand side was the village of Alness and, further along, Invergordon, where the RAF deployed a Marine Craft Unit, and MBC (motorboat crew) attended their sea-going target-towing launch (TTL), which, during night-time manoeuvres, towed an underwater facsimile of a submarine periscope. At speed, pulling the partly submerged object, disturbed water resembled the telltale direction of the submarine. Shackleton aircraft from Lossiemouth or Kinloss would track the TTL and drop flares (instead of explosive depth charges) on either side of the moving target.

I volunteered for one night's bombing exercise but was advised to stay below deck because the "splashes" from the mock bombs inundated the hastening craft. In fact, I fell asleep and was woken up after the night raid exercise was over.

Crew members related that during other night exercises, one pilot was spot-on target and blew up the submerged object, and was not a popular buddy!

Not long after we climbed Fyrish, two walkers were killed near where we had been. Unseen, a warning noticeboard, "Keep to the paths. Beware of unmarked edges," was missing. They must have fallen hundreds of feet to their deaths, and the area was "out of bounds" for a while.

Climbing was a demanding, physically strenuous, energy-sapping challenge, to which you had to keep to designated pathways.

It was a shock to think we had walked the same path!

To our right, Evanton was once an airfield and a motor circuit. Sundays it was open to drivers owning sports cars of the time and made interesting and sometimes hair-raising incidents when speeding cars spun off and headed towards the crowds eagerly watching the racing. Keen auto designers with their own home-made models were no match for professional whizzkids in open-cockpit Lotuses, adapted Fords and three-wheelers, which skidded and made tyres squeal. Hot metal and oil smells, along with additional additive-induced fumes, held in the cold, abrupt morning air. Cars, by today's standards, without servo-assisted brakes, four-wheel drive, or special gearboxes, were driven by young and advanced, experienced men and women, with eager anticipation, nerves of steel, and flew round the circuit like mad agitated ants. Speed was exciting, heart rate pounded.

Assorted headgear included deerstalkers, Avon fibreglass helmets; one young chap wore an ex-USA highway police officer's headwear, which drew lots of attention, but most wore robber-style balaclavas; a few had woolly hats, and a couple of berets were seen. Ancient three-wheeled Morgans' exhausts smoked after a few laps, and the sound was awesome!

The only fault of the day—it was so cold, especially standing in the same spot. There were no catering facilities either.

I am not a hundred per cent certain, but they also had motorcycle and scooter races. No doubt nowadays it is a weekend farmers' market, spaced out similarly, or would be an excellent car boot sale site.

A nearby stream leading into a river, then the Cromarty Firth, was where I saw my first kingfisher. Have not seen one since!

As a family, we travelled (twice) on The Royal Highlander, at the time the longest single train journey in the UK.

A sleeper, and wonderfully comfortable, started out from London Euston railway station to Inverness, capital of The Highlands.

We spent two terrific years, with marvellous scenery and pure, fresh air. Discovered stovies, scrumptious meat pies, and went over the Forth railway bridge before the 'new one' was built. Briefly halting at Culloden Moor. The vista of this historic battleground looked featureless. I peered out a window as we stopped and was aware of the silence…. no birds, no wind sighs, it was eerie. Nearby, an open-air curling game was seen for the first time. It looked sedate, calm but intense. This was the year President John F. Kennedy was assassinated.

1986

I worked as the only full-time male toilet attendant for over four tedious, strenuous, stressful years in underground public conveniences, now storage for the 'dancing fountains' machinery with no visible proof of its existence. These innocent remarks were passed from son to parent while using the facility, overheard when in my little 'office', in summer months. Smiles galore.

"You are silly, the cleaning man doesn't live in that cupboard."

"No, the flushing water is not for cleaning our shoes."

"Your sister cannot come down here, silly boy."

"Stop looking at that man, it's rude."

"I don't know how many tiles are on the wall, you count them."

"What have you been eating? You stink."

"No, I don't think men sleep in the cubicles."

"You can't eat chips down here, stupid."

"I don't know if granddad comes here, you'll have to ask him."

"Watch where you're weeing, they are new socks."

"Don't bring ice cream in here, nutter."

"You'll have to find your shoes before we go home."

You would hear mothers while watching their kids go down the concrete steps into the toilets shout down, "Hurry up and don't talk to anyone," as if something horrible was going to happen. There was always a dubious element associated with toilets.

A few minutes before closing, a young curly-haired mixed-race teenager hurriedly brought an enormous bunch of flowers and sat in one of the cubicles. I was about to shut the gates. He said, "I nicked these from a shop, you won't tell on me, will you?" There was always a last-minute dash to the bogs before closing. You could bet on it. I had turned off the lighting, and the place was in darkness.

As sure as eggs is eggs, awkward sods yelled, "Don't shut, mister, we're dying for a piss," with grins on faces, unzipping themselves as they headed down into the bowels of the earth.

There were disgusting, filthy, dirty episodes which are not suitable to describe, and the question of "How on earth are these people allowed out in public?" went through my mind many times at the state they left the sit-downs.

Good thing I had a cast-iron stomach. I care not to mention, as many despicable acts cannot be related for public decency's sake, were encountered. It was sickening, to say the least. All part of a toilet attendant's job! I could not ask someone else to clean up, could I? Really sick mental nut cases. Not everyone would survive the day-to-day demands within a council-run service because of many aspects to maintain the cleanliness of such a misaligned vital factor associated with public needs. It was, and is, an important part of everyday requirements, but people abuse and look down on staff maintaining this necessary facility. I was extremely angry at patrons who ignored a simple thing as pulling the chain after using the sit-downs. There were certainly oddballs in our midst.

For years, there has never been acknowledgement of how important toilets were/are. People cannot live without a decent, well-kept, clean toilet.

Ask anyone; they will say, "Never really thought about it," which hits the nail exactly on its head. No one understands the back-room business towards a natural function as going to the toilet. They do not wish to know. Simple as that!

When people complain about their dull, uninteresting office job or such, I can honestly say without fear of contradiction, "I TRULY HAD A CRAP JOB."

High up above a urinal, written in red italic marker pen, was the message, "If you are looking at this, you are pissing down your trousers."

One quiet off-season afternoon, I decided to block off one side of the men's toilet to apply a chemical used for unblocking drains, for something to do.

Placed cones across part of the entrance so silly sods could not walk where I was mopping. There were times I wanted to scream when having cleaned the complete floor area (floor was wet, OK?).

What happens? Mr Proper Silly Arsehole moved a cone and treaded on the wet marbled floor. A sign should have warned him: DANGER, wet area, use other urinals.

Meanwhile, I add cold water to the mop container, in seconds, a frothy white mist-like cloud erupts and suddenly, worryingly, flows out from the bucket.

I drop the incredibly obnoxious mixture to the floor entrance and hurriedly make my way up the steps to get fresh air. The mystery foam smells so strong it brings tears to my eyes. Reaching the top of the stairs and looking back down into the toilet, the foam spread over the concrete and up the first two steps. I am horrified and afraid to have done something extremely dangerous. Suddenly, three gents in suits approach. I stop them walking down the steps and explain. One man, a supervisor for a commercial maintenance company, remarks, according to his experience (and sense of smell), that I mixed two chemicals, and the foam fumes could harm the respiratory system. It had to be washed away quickly before members of the public became victims of its caustic power. That was the only time I mixed chemicals. Considering the seriousness and brief time it happened, I was exceptionally lucky, as was anyone in its vicinity. It could have caused serious health issues, even death (according to the man). Bloody stroll on. I only wanted to flush the urinals... not cause a public disaster! Hell no!

I threatened to close the bogs during busy summer weekends in demonstration towards a pay claim we had put forward for all toilet attendants. One lady attendant and I went to our head office in Norwich and spent an hour relating circumstances associated with management, daily abuse, equipment issues and closing times. Might as well have not bothered; nothing was done.

Ironically, after I gave notice to leave the shitty, piss-awful job, members of staff did get their pay rise. Service life sustained speaking up for myself because I loathed unfairness or neglect towards industrious colleagues, resented being looked down upon or being taken for granted.

Having to listen to new petty rules and regulations from younger managerial staff and being asked, "Why did you want ten toilet chains with the weekly commodity demand?"

"BECAUSE NASTY LITTLE GITS REMOVED THEM WHILE I WAS HAVING A DINNER BREAK". That was the reason, moron!

The thought of youngsters deliberately looking out for me was alarming.

I was fed up to the teeth with monotony, and this was serious.

During freezing cold winter months, not a single person entered. Storm-blown sand was continuously swept from the stairs in case a member of the public might slip over. Also, removing human excreta deposited on the lower four steps was gross and degrading. People used the place as a shithouse whether it was closed or not. It was overwhelming; I began hating what I was doing day in, day out, week upon week. Felt belittled and thoroughly pissed off. Willingly, I signed my termination of employment with the then local council. I was totally disheartened after four years of hard labour.

This is, as far as I am aware, the only written document relating to the toilets, and I have been told that this text is now an historic document. Which it is, of course! Who else had the experience to do something as odd as documenting a seaside underground bog?

One day's work at McDonald's in town as the oldest crew member was enough. The interior heat was felt as soon as I walked in. Could not breathe.

Every rock-hard frozen product was timed to the second, and high-pitched buzzers went off constantly. The repetitiveness of cooking each item, plus the lingering odours of cooking oils, resulted in thoughts of "You will not stay long in this job, matey." The uniform given was far too tight for my mature figure. Anyway, I did not like their products, which we ate for lunch.

In those bygone days, you could readily visit the job centre, who stamped a chitty, gave you a list of vacancies, choose one favoured, and off you jolly well went to see if it were fitting and enjoyable. A moon's journey from current requirements.

Spotting an advert on a Co-op supermarket "For Sale" board, I took the telephone number and spoke to a lady receptionist. There were two temporary positions to fill. That is great, I immediately thought.

I knew the venue because they had themed cabarets, well-known bands played there, and the place was immensely popular with older folk.

During summer, queues of visiting buses lined up beside the dance floor.

Hundreds of holidaymakers swarmed for the Christmas weekends and novelty nights.

I became a general assistant in an out-of-season holiday village, where I cleaned, scraped, sweated, and swore at the previous season's used pots, pans, and serving utensils (by the unwashed dozen). This was on a Friday. Tuesday, I was in another position.

Security officer on short-term contracts came next. One on a remote rural site. Tall metal fencing topped with curly barbed wire encapsulated an area the size of a football pitch. Security lights on each corner, and in the centre of the grass and concreted area (under a lamp on a pole) was a white-painted plastic-windowed hut, parked on wooden pallets. It was so small, hardly any room to move, with an uncomfortable wooden stool that had extended legs. A wind-up alarm clock stared back at me on a narrow window ledge. I sat in the tiny hut with grass peeping through each floor bar, and an electric single-bar convector heater for heat against the cold. Overhead lighting attracted lots of moths, and an owl head-butted the window. That made me jump. Did crossword puzzles to keep awake. Lorry drivers came through the gates, neatly parked, approached the hut and signed a diary-like, well-used book.

There was seldom any movement of trucks until around ten or eleven at night, with one or two early morning arrivals. There were never more than six HGVs parked each evening during my three weeks there.

I watched water droplets slowly slide down the plastic window as if in a hidden race. It constantly misted up, and my feet were cold for three weeks after I left. The only good point of the shift work was the wages. I must have been raving mental.

Second appointment within security was much better. Part of a commercial trading estate containing a car dismantling yard, paint distribution outlet, a box-making company, steel fabrication works and workshops. Again, I volunteered for nights and wore a heavy military-type jacket when checking ten outdoor locks on massive metal doors to hangar-sized units. The only orders I had were to stagger patrol times and alter the route.

That was for five nights only but I enjoyed what I was doing. Tea/coffee was available, as the adjacent room was part of a canteen facility. (I had the keys.) A decent relaxing job. Now and again, bosses rang to see if everything was OK. Or to check up on me?

"Why am I fed up when walking in the recycling yard?" "That shows you are down in the dumps." The reply.

"Do you say the yolk of an egg is white or are white?"

"White, surely?"

"No, you are wrong, the yolk of an egg is YELLOW."

A boy stood on the burning deck, picking his nose like mad, he rolled them up in little balls and flicked them at his dad.

Two Irish mates. Tam asked Patrick, "How do you spell paint?" Patrick replied, "What colour?"

From a building in Thorpe Road next to the railway station in Norwich, five applicants were handed a typewritten script with attached business cards. This was senseless, extremely cold and of no interest to the public, attempting to sell insurance (cold calling) not far from the busy marketplace. After two hours of rejection, no potential purchases, I bade goodbye and returned the cards, seeing two of the other bods having a smoke outside the white-painted building. They said the same as me, "F...k that for a game of soldiers, I can't feel my feet." Having read off the brief script repeatedly to all and sundry, on what must have been the coldest day of the year, was thankless beyond words. How did anyone make a living from walking the streets?

If we go shopping in Norwich, which is not often, I remember the short-lasting footslogging two hours spent in the busiest city in Norfolk. It was chronic!

On the rear window of a grand old black Ford Zephyr Mark Three, I had a rectangular stick-on logo created in the USA, which was given to me when buying petrol from a garage near Aylsham (a long time ago), which made passers-by smile. I have not seen another like it anywhere. This was in the late sixties/early seventies. It declared, "I WOULD RATHER EAT WORMS THAN DRIVE A FORD." Quite a statement? I owned that car for ten years and, when it failed an MOT, stripped out most ancillaries and advertised Parts for Sale in a local newspaper.

It was incredibly successful. I sold both doors to a father and son from Lincolnshire. The large ornate steering wheel and horn ring went to a young man who raced stock cars at Great Yarmouth. The entire brake system, piping included, went along with axle stands, hydraulic jacks, headlights and wiring system, both front and rear seats, even the headlining eventually sold, leaving a ransacked shell, and I had to pay to have it taken away to a scrapyard.

I kept the number plate for years — 81 EER.

My first motor was a Hillman Husky, which I hand-painted with beige Valspar paint. Had to add an end exhaust tailpipe and a battery, pumped up the tyres and sold it for £75. I was twenty.

A corporal airman who lived three doors away at RAF married quarters at Wyton, Huntingdonshire, was being posted overseas, and I bought his elderly Ford Popular 100E, Ambassador blue, with a wobbly gearstick and a silly windscreen wiper system. Did lots of miles around Cambridgeshire, including St Ives, Huntingdon, Ramsey Abbey, Warboys, Peterborough, and the Hemingfords, an extremely attractive series of picturesque villages. It was hellishly frustrating trying to park in Cambridge. Hated shopping there. The number of cycles was bewildering AND they rode without care for the crowded city roads or pedestrians. Silly prats!

In Peterborough, before every town had them, a Mr Brierly ran the first supermarket and served customers, giving young kids sweets. He was the local millionaire who would chat and have a laugh. You would never know he had money. Would wear an apron even at the tills. Did not know much about him.

I drove a collection of cars, and memories eternally live on. They include a Cortina Mark One, short-wheelbase uncomfortable noisy, ex-military police patrol Land Rover. A three-wheeler Bond. Another ex-military staff car (only drove it to park) a huge Humber Snipe. A35 van. Hillman Imp. Ford 105E with sloping rear screen, in which I passed my driving test on the second go. Ford Fiesta 997cc OHV model. On our way to Nottinghamshire with hills, we were overtaken by lorries ascending several inclines. Owned it for ten years.

I loved a TR7 but spent more than an arm and a leg replacing most parts, including tyres and brakes. Two Mark Three Cortinas, one 1600 and one 2000 XL. Ford Zodiac Mark Three Automatic. One Ford Focus and two Escorts.

Currently, I run a Ford Series 2 Ka. Low mileage, one lady owner. Ideally, I would like a limousine with every bell and whistle, soft suspension, front and rear cameras and in-car entertainment. Super. No sunroof! Nearly forgot, a Ford D1100 Trainee Driver HGV lorry with a thirty-foot trailer, in which I drove through Norwich during my second lesson. I failed that test. Sweat buckets. Getting down from the cab, a shadow-like patch on the seat and backrest was from the concentration and effort given. I still have the provisional black licence.

As a point of interest, a spotless red BSA 250cc C15 model like the one I briefly owned recently sold for over £6,000. Blimey! I prefer old British bikes to whizz-bangs. Ended my motorcycling days with a great little BSA C12, which would just nudge 75 miles per hour with a wind behind me. URT 75. It was a C11 G to be perfectly correct, with overhead valves, not a side-valve model!

Approaching the King's Lynn Hardwick roundabout at night, a rear tyre blew out. Driving a Cotton Continental Villiers two-stroke twin-cylinder sports motorcycle, painted bright yellow, lots of chrome and a mini flyscreen, I lost my nerve and did not sit on a motorcycle for many years.

When changing clothes back at camp, I found out I had messed myself. The shock of coming off the bike went straight through me. The Stadium Cruiser skid lid (helmet) split when hitting the roadway, one ball-end lever grip was vertically bent, and a handlebar-end mirror was smashed. Apart from that, I was fine. Dizzy but fine. Prior to the scene of the 'accident', a lorry driver witnessed me skid across the road and considered, "You were f..king lucky, mate." He was only yards behind me; his headlights saw me roll down a grass incline along the highway. I surely was lucky. That evening, I had one incessant throbbing headache, my right arm ached, and the riding jacket (not a Barbour) split from neck to waist.

Months later, my ex-father-in-law, George Copsey, said he had a surprise for me, and it was arriving next Sunday sometime after lunch.

He had already bought me the Ford Zodiac automatic from a market in Swaffham. It was a non-runner. We bought a battery, used jump leads and, incredibly, it started up in seconds.

The surprise in the back of an Austin pickup was a unique black Panther 600 cc motorcycle with side-car attachments, which we ditched, did not need them. Single cylinder, but twin exhaust pipes sprouted from the engine unit.

For three weeks, I oiled and removed all parts, labelled and stored them in boxes, cleaned, brushed, scraped, and fiddled, adjusted and polished, for later, to be assembled and put together. That, however, was not forthcoming. A bombshell ruined the future of a complete renovation of the wonderful bike. I WAS POSTED TO ANOTHER RAF STATION. I was stupefied. Bugger.

At least things worked out. George knew the father of a mechanic that worked in Peter Bacon's garage/shop in Swaffham. He repaired cars and motorcycles. At least it was going to be resurrected by someone that knew what he was doing!

That motorcycle model is, as older bikes of that era are, now worth several thousand pounds. Wow! To think I took one apart, how frightening is that? I could easily take things to bits, but it was a miracle if all parts refitted correctly. That was me. I always learnt from mistakes!

Of the hundreds of people I briefly met or spoke to in the car parks, toilets or other employments, a few would be known to the public.

It was genuinely nice and exciting to see television stars in the flesh, let alone speak to them. One Saturday mid-morning, on the top-most parking level of Battery Green multi-storey, Stratford Johns of Z-Cars fame was waiting for his wife, who had gone shopping. He was parked in a Suzuki Jeep. I had my 'booking pad' in my hand, as you do, and walked over to him.

He smiled, said, "My wife won't be long, spending my hard-earned money as usual," and chatted a couple of minutes about what he was doing.

They were looking forward to a long-planned holiday.

I wished him good luck, although my powers of observation recognised the fact he did not have a ticket. I could not book him, could I?

What do you call a three-humped camel? HUMPHREY

Another day, about to write down details of a brown Volvo estate (it had exceeded its period of parking) when a voice called out, "I'm here." It was Bob Blizzard, the local MP. "Got held up in a meeting." I smiled and remarked, "Good job you turned up." On a summer afternoon, Andy de la Tour, brother of actress Frances de la Tour, visited the toilets. I asked was he busy, to which he replied, "I'm appearing in a show, down the coast." That was it, and he disappeared up the stairs into sunlight.

One mid-morning on level four of Battery Green, television personality, world traveller and reporter, the man in the white suit, Martin Bell, emerged from a car containing two smartly dressed gents. As usual, to all customers, I said a polite "Good morning" and was totally snubbed. I was only a car parks inspector, not worth replying to, and took an instant dislike to the man. To this day, whenever he appears on TV, I point out, "That's the snooty git that didn't notice me." Sod him.

Parked on the top level of the same multi-storey car park, late in the afternoon, getting ready to finish work for the day, a gleaming Rolls-Royce beckoned my approach. It had no parking ticket displayed. I gave it the allowed ten minutes' grace, then booked it. Was later told by an office staff member it was owned by Jack Smethurst of *Love Thy Neighbour* fame. He was appearing at the Marina Theatre that evening.

I glimpsed the one-time British heavyweight boxing champion Joe Bugner, refuelling his gold-coloured Volvo two-seat sports car at a St Ives, Cambridgeshire, garage, long before he decided to live in Australia. His wife was so tiny in comparison to his stature.

"Ivanhoe... Ivanhoe... I've a rake… I've a shovel... Ivanhoe."

"I met a charming foreign lady named Isabelle Font… but she was not my type!"

I found five car park inspector notebooks going through a collection of birthday cards. Every page was scrawled, oops, carefully written details of each vehicle that had broken parking rules. It was a shock to scan hundreds and hundreds of cars. Must have been truly dedicated to my job, because on the last page of my final patrol (having added all month-by-month totals together) I had 'booked' over twenty-four thousand vehicles. The date was September 30th 2000, all that revenue, didn't I do well?

All that extra council revenue, I bet they missed me when I left.

I did write lots of extra information in case of discrepancies with those folks who queried the £60 fine. Lots of fines were queried and cancelled. Cannot win them all, eh? Little factors such as a moped road tax disc on a Vauxhall Viva. Disabled driver's badge a year out of date. Motorcycles parked in trolley bays. Restricted parking with an all-day ticket. Continental drivers thought car parks were free. And a homemade tax disc on a Renault. They try to get away from paying a parking fee, then argue the toss when a yellow ticket is found under their windscreen wiper. Tearing up the ticket did not help at all, because the original was left on my little black notepad. It was amusing when visitors displayed multiple outdated tickets from other seaside counties.

Parking prices and wage facts were perused. My title was Enforcement Officer. £11,838–£14,391 pa. Tuesdays off but worked Bank Holidays. Monthly permits £22.50. Quarterly permits £63.00. Parking fees were 40p per hour, 80p two hours, £1.20 3 hours, £1.60 4 hours, over 4 hours £2.20 and overnight parking only 40p.

Prices certainly increased since then, but I have no up-to-date data.

During the writing of this, one of the two multi-storey car parks has been demolished to make way for a multi-function, multi-million-pound town centre cultural centre with café, pop-up bars, a studio, leisure facilities and three landmark buildings. Golly. Gosh. However, nothing is indicated about new toilets, which was and still is a vital issue. Sounds about right! Half of my workplace no longer exists. May ghosts of my thousands of footsteps up, down and across the once vital multi-storey building be forever patrolling, watching out for non-paying clients.

Over many years, beautiful, functional old buildings were indiscriminately pulled down, with no thought of retaining their character or potential re-usage for posterity. Local council committees never considered the public's concern for eradicating once-splendid edifices of architectural value which could have easily been given facelifts or renovation, not blatant vandalism!

Long-gone industries could have been saved, instead of over-zealous non-residential personages being given permission to obliterate reusable constructions. It was sad! The area known as The Beach could have been kept for future generations to see the squalid cramped conditions of cottages and shops, but no, council powers in charge bulldozed and flattened every individual property, without foresight to create what might have been a wonderful sightseeing village relic. Non-residents would never believe how squalid housing conditions were before the great flood!

There was no vision to preserve historic buildings or workplaces that could have been a money-earner towards holiday trade. There are vacant plots of land where, years ago, fisherfolk attempted to make a living in dire, unhealthy, inadequate conditions.

So much could have been done, but sweet f..k all resulted. As usual!

I always felt strongly about my previous home and others in the area. The Beach should have been retained as it was, no fancy decorative embellishments, no modernisation, double glazing, tarting up and spoiling original cottages, pubs, stores, commercial premises; left as it was basic, not interfered with unhealthy sub-standard accommodation, where families of hard-working fisherfolk existed within their own close-knit community. It would have been a wonderful idea to have retained several original homes, including the pubs, parking yards for lorries and a few hundred fish barrels for effect, such as York, but no, the entire area was flattened and forgotten for future industrial purposes.

Any Seaside in November

It is strangely empty of milling throngs,

no noise of jukebox top twenty songs

Summers' hectic commerciality sleeps

as rain pours endlessly down the streets.

Hotels, cafes are warm but complacent.

atmosphere is cold dull and vacant.

Amusement arcades all bright with plastic,

without murmur fervour, the event seldom drastic.

Pavements reflections a mirror-like sheen,

immaculate gardens trimmed vivid green.

Wind and the coldness constantly pester,

an annoying, boring fact, without fiesta.

Passing traffic disturbing the peace

is the only thing moving, not given to cease.

To mad-cap August and visitors it dreams

to cater for hunger and new colour schemes.

Thousands of portions of delicious fish n chips,

winkles and cockles, salty air on lips.

Strangely empty of milling throngs,

no loud top twenty jukebox songs

Summer's hectic commerciality sleeps,

as rain pours endlessly down seaside streets

Why did a middle-aged spinster buy lots of colourful lovebirds?

Because she couldn't get a cockatoo!

Why was the midget transsexual feeling sad? He was a bit of a drag.

Why did the camper get arrested? Because he was fighting within tent.

A cuckoo clock got hiccups and could not control the burps,

no matter how many preventatives, ended up gargling with turps.

After two days in hospital, I took a turn for a nurse (W. C. Fields)

There are mice in houses, rats in flats, wriggling things in offices,

spiders' webs by the dozen, with tiny insects in hidden orifices.

Silverfish, cockroaches, bedbugs too, mysterious fluff bundles under the loo.

Ants and fleas and sometimes bees bring mates to have a laugh.

You cannot see them, but they're there, watching you having a bath.

Yonks ago, a teenage fad was writing notes from girlfriend to boyfriend, vice versa, that perpetuated for ages. You added INITIALS on the back of envelopes with innocent phrases disguised as sexual content. Funny and mischievous, it sparked adolescent dreams of their ideal boy/girl but was never meant in seriousness.

ELY was Ever Loving You.

BOLTOP: Better On Lips Than On Paper.

ITALY: I Trust And Love You.

EGYPT: Ever Grasp Your Precious Tits.

BURMA: Be Undressed Ready My Angel.

HOLLAND: Hope Our Love Lasts And Never Dies.

SIAM: Sexual Intercourse After Midnight.

CAPSTAN: Can A Prick Stand Twice A Night?

NORWICH: (K)nickers Off Ready When I Come Home.

NAAFI: Navy, Army, Air Force Institute. The forces' own Tesco/ASDA/Co-op...

suppliers to all military outlets.

Also known as... No Ambition And F..k All Interest. Oh dear!

Each military camp/ship/station ran a NAAFI shop supplying married quarters.

An essential outlet for all personnel, civvy and airmen.

Met a guy with a glass eye, he didn't tell me, it just came out during

conversation. (Jerry Dennis)

A kleptomaniac is a person that helps himself because he cannot help himself.

(Henry Morgan)

'It might not be the wrong word that hurts, it's how it is said.' Anon.

'The longest journey begins with one step.' (Chinese proverb)

Recovering from a Polyp Removal Operation 2010

Did the sun rise today? Is it February or May?

Because I never saw its bright splendour, why?

Sedated, warm, numb that comforting unseen sun.

Seagulls dived and screeched close by,

to the background of a greying sky.

External smells lingered, causing nausea,

my head spun and mouth dry.

Medical whiffs, bleach, cleaning vapours drifted by my bed.

Detected urine as older male patients passed, smiled. I nodded my head.

Was the weather on a go-slow, had the sun gone abroad for a break?

What will be on the menu tomorrow? Bet it is not onions with steak.

Feet feel leaden, my legs the same,

tingling fingertips. Will I fully recover again?

Smells and feelings lingered too long, I wanted an ice-cold beer.

Stomach rumbled. When last did I eat, and wished to get out from here.

Sleep hastens further concentration. Where did the sun go (away)?

Heavy eyes are too demanding. Let me sleep for the rest of the day.

From a preliminary medical examination, it was a shock to be told I had three cancer polyps within the lower section of my large intestine (right hemi-colectomy). Successfully removed, was given the 'all clear'. After five years' COPD observation, my lung condition is Bronchiectasis. Treatable with no physical symptoms or pain! Thank heavens! Since a tiny child, plagued by wheezing, congested lungs, nasty asthma, many nights my head was stuck out of windows to inhale fresh air instead of allergic interiors. Many things triggered an attack when it felt like breathing through a straw. Bleach, paint, ash from open fires, all sorts of smoke. A few flowers like lavender easily made me sneeze, flour (cooking), and some perfumes! Hell!

The Thing in the Shed

There's an odd misshapen old thing held together by pieces of string on the back of a shelf near a broken garden elf, next to a rusty bedspring. It is not a gruesome ugly sight; I would prefer it coloured bright gloss white.

Admittedly, it's seen better days, under a multitude of flowerbed trays.

But it always looks not right.

Grandfather owned it, mother said, kept it beneath his feather bed,

used it as a Sunday hat on his head.

The man that drove the baker's van (the man that lived in a caravan)

took it up on the vicar's roof tiles, where it could be seen from many miles,

and in a moment of disbelief, fell to the ground just like an autumn leaf.

It's been placed on garden walls, thrown, and kicked on Sunday footballs.

Left on banks of streams and rivers, caused many worrying shakes and shivers,

never has the object been drowned, it is a mystery where it was originally found.

The Mayor of Leicester wrote it a note. Been taken to sea in a fisherman's boat.

Used as a mop when rain poured down, was nailed to a door of The Rose and Crown.

The thing behind the door in the garden shed has been there since Mr Brown was found

dead.

His children want it made into a nice big garden shade.

Until someone finds a spot, let the thing in the shed stay there to rot.

I sent a lot of poetry to well-known publishing companies, without one appreciative acknowledgement in return. No advice on titles or content of compositions, no constructive hints, not even a rejection slip. Zero! What has an aspiring writer/poet to do to improve or amend samples of their efforts towards publication? Answers on a postcard, please. When answering a question like "What hobbies have you got?" and the reply is "I WRITE." Half-heartedly, wide-eyed, and aghast, they continue, "Is that all?" I spend more time writing in the back bedroom, which is our study, than being with my wife, who is downstairs. I feel selfish, not sitting with her. My eyes blink continuously as I stare at the screen, twenty-four inches in front of me. Mouth gets dry and get painful cramps in my legs.

When I get a reply like that, I want to scream, "You try it!" Even at my age I have ambition, bugger off, leave me alone!"

I sent the next poem to one of many 'subsidy' publishers. Did not enclose the subscription fee, so they never entered it. Now I know how they get their money. Admittedly, have relied upon this system to enable the first few efforts into paperback to give evidence of my creative genius to the public.

A Derelict Country House

Previous residents have long gone.

No daily routine here, no opening doors give warning of intrusion, within bare spider-web adorned rooms. No noise except wind sighs sneaking through broken windows that once shone like excited children's eyes, down lofty chimneys into open brick and flint fireplaces.

Dust appoints itself governor of the derelict house, fulfilling a lifetime ambition of ownership. Haloed by the sun's bright illumination, specks spiral lazily upwards, unconcerned at the silence. Spiders examine the vacant kingdom, accepting the delightfully cosy acquisition. More scurrying insects race throughout the grime. Ghost memories yearn for company since former owners left the country home.

As a delivery driver for a FORD retail garage, I took spares, oil, gearboxes, metal panels, etc., for commercial and domestic vehicles as far as Cromer. On my last country drop, I would sweep out the Transit van, ensure returns were in their boxes, lock the rear door and prepare for the return journey. I would make notes on where I was parked and glance round to see if anything of interest was nearby.

This occasion, a large Victorian house on its own, behind tall untidy bushes, was close to the main road. Hurriedly wrote loose descriptive notes on what I could see and would add details later. In winter months it was no fun, but during summer sunshine and clear skies, I wrote much prose/poems coming back from north Norfolk. East Anglia contains wonderful old buildings, and it's my duty to describe the ones I saw. It is sorrowful to see lovely family homes in partial ruins throughout each county, requiring complete modernisation to become once again lived in and be utilised for the use they were built! It is sad that thousands of once superb buildings are left to nature's harsh demands.

I have great sympathy and compassion towards buildings, no matter size, shape or purpose, left to gradually fall into a state of disrepair. It is a crime allowing old structures such as farm buildings, mills (wind and water), hospitals, churches, schools, to fall to pieces brick by brick until nothing can be done to bring back life into a dying dwelling. There should be a government white paper ensuring this practice is illegal and owners responsible for the neglect should be given unlimited community service (working on run-down dilapidated buildings). So there. Next effort has similar content. Based on a 'Land Registry & Regulation' document and a court case, the result was (in non-technical jargon) current owners were instructed to rebuild, maintain and facilitate to good standards the building, outbuildings, water garden and folly (with a small obelisk) and it is a popular family attraction, mainly during summer months.

A very fine bird is a Pelican, his beak holds more than his belly can.

Why are fish excellent singers? They know all the scales.

An Aesthetic Delight

A fine country house with black gable ends, pink-washed plaster, brick and flint frontage, stands amid a cluttered garden that glows with a profusion of flowers and shrubs. A wide gravelled path crunches each stride underfoot against riding boots, leather shoe soles or soft feathery slippers, on after-tea strolls around showy beds of tall, swaying, delicate grass and fern.

A splendid rockery borders a slow-moving shallow stream with darting 'get-out-of-my-way' miniature fish, are talking points by ambling parasol-carrying ladies and pipe-smoking trilby-wearing gents. With grumpy anti-walking, stone-kicking boys making faces at sisters, lagging paces behind. Parents miles ahead ignore them. The garden was transformed from formal, regimented lines with an occasional curve, into somewhere peaceful to wander unconcerned, admire tall willow trees bowing and swaying to a thought of a breeze. Less tall plantage shivers as swans regally disturb the reeds and pass through, heads up and aloof.

Everything in the garden was fine, in fact. Nature's gifts of colour, scent, beauty, all in abundance. The only noise interrupting the idyllic scene comes from a pair of agitated, disgruntled peacocks. Garishly coloured chickens scurry about, stop and peck at something only they see. Pigeons circle and drop in a mass display of formation flying. Grunting pigs behind a waist-high wall make squelching sounds treading in a clay-like substance, noses half-buried in the shitty-looking mass. Someone's dog yelps as a man in dark glasses shuts metal gates (the dog half-way through). Heads turned. All's well. On to the café for a cake.

Honeymoon, the morning after the KNOT before (Anon)

Anybody that goes to see a psychiatrist ought to have their head seen to. (Sam Goldwyn)

Malt extract was an everyday dosage during wintry schooldays, with a "It will do you good and protect from colds" from an ever-fussing mother. Two spoonfuls after cereals or toast. There were two flavours, and cod-liver oil left the mouth with a fishy taste all day. The sweet one was called Maltlene. It can still be bought under a new company name.

November 18th 1999
From 01.17 am until 01.38 am

Watching the unique Tempel-Tuttle comet.

I was proud to have seen this remarkable spectacle.

I stood against the sun lounge door in a near-freezing temperature,

the sky a perfect blackboard background.

Wore normal casual clothes. Saw breath in the air. There was no sound.

My eyes slowly acclimatised to the above distant view. I shivered.

Suddenly, unannounced, a speeding meteor tail whizzed across my line of

vision as quick as a wink. Then others followed at the same speed.

I had never seen so many split-second fragments of colour in the sky. My eyes

watered at the cold. Feet were frozen, neck ached. Was aware I had slippers on.

The endless spectacle was from a science-fiction film, amazing, very special.

The number of speeding-coloured objects was fun. Inwardly I smiled.

A serious question developed: where were they heading, to what finality,

zooming through the atmosphere at 158,000 miles per hour, sixty miles above

Earth?

Dribbling eyes wilted from constant squinting at the rare demonstration.

My clothes were cold. Numb feet hinted to go indoors to bed and sleep.

Had my heart rate increased in awe, must have?

Pleased to have witnessed the Tempel-Tuttle comet. I would not see it a second

time. (This cosmic snowstorm appears in thirty-three-year cycles.)

Beyond Childhood

During whistling, holes-in-trousers childhood

we happily enjoyed ourselves in simplistic innocence.

Walked those pre-responsibility days with ease,

and kicked happiness in all directions.

We long for such unashamed, innocent hours

when we talked to friends about everything we knew

and threw stones and sticks into mirrored ponds and pools.

We could not see our future spread out as rings in the water spread out.

Nor could we imagine difficulties in our virginity.

The water is still there... unaffected, our whistling has changed tune,

friends have passed on as our treasured childhood passed on,

but where did simplicity and enjoyment disappear to?

We played 'flickies' with cigarette cards. These were placed against a wall, and the person whose card knocked it down took the card or cards. I fail to recall names, but there were lots of card games and marbles, skipping, rounders, rope climbing and, in winter, a long sloping slippery slide was popular for those who dared to skid along it. Swapping cards of sports competitors of the era was excitably enthusiastic, and serious exchanges had to be supervised by the duty teacher in the playground.

In late 1950s, conkers were an amusing, intense introduction to competitions around playgrounds, but lots of minor injuries were associated with the so-called safe game as the shells shattered and flew everywhere, including into the eyes of players. Kicking a hard leather football against walls was commonplace. Girls preferred hopscotch, skipping, hand games with odd names.

Leapfrog showed how well you could jump over bent-in-half bodies of mates, and even then, there were failures and two children ended up on the concrete.

Peashooters were so popular that the headteacher prevented older boys from bringing them into school. Another short-lasting fad was the really dreaded metal catapults, they could be dangerous if using tiny ammunition such as ball bearings. That was scary indeed.

Horsey Mill

Near Waxham, north Norfolk.

Horsey Mill, Horsey Mill, how long the time your sails are still?

You look out over nothing land. Cow-favoured, flat, peculiarly bland.

Not too beautiful but has romance. A river behind your charming stance.

Decades of winds, storms, and weather, few birds, grass and sparse of heather.

Horsey Mill, Horsey Mill, a fleeting glance, a silent thrill.

Cow-favoured, flat, bordering bland. You look out over nothing grand.

Your antiquity is worth a hundred smiles, as eternally, you watch the watery

miles.

Do As I Say Not As I Do

An over-protective father tells his young son how to dress properly,

tie laces, comb his hair, and how to conduct himself when in public places.

Not to be cruel to animals, talk politely to older people and be helpful

when asked. How to eat and not talk with food in his mouth,

encourages him to be better than he was at his age.

To respect his mother and lays a comforting arm around the frail pre-adolescent

lad's shoulders.

The father goes out for the evening.

Gets drunk. Is sick over someone's garden wall. Pushes over dustbins.

Pulls flowers from a pensioner's bungalow window box. Urinates against

a fence bordering a path beside the bungalow. Shouts abuse to passing cyclists.

Phones an ex-lady friend... there is no reply... punches the glass telephone kiosk

door. Makes suggestive remarks to a couple waiting for a bus.

Arriving back home, cooks bacon, sausage, and fried potatoes until blue smoke

from the frying pan activates an alarm.

Leaves a greasy plate on the kitchen table.

Throws shoes across the room and puts stinking socks on the banister rail.

Tottering into the bedroom, discarding his clothes, wakes his half-asleep shift-worker wife, who must give in to his conjugal rights. Endures his grunting, thrusting, until he selfishly satisfies himself to an accompaniment of squeaking, creaking loose bedsprings. He turns over, belches, farts and falls into a hazy slumber.

Sleeps until midday. Walks naked to wash his hair, splashing nearby surfaces. Swills his teeth, visits the bathroom, does not pull the chain. Slams shut the cupboard door in which he selects another set of clothes. Smartens himself up to go to Chapman's the bookies, where he stays until tea time until one of his mates remarks about a new pub opening, "You ready or not?"

My younger years contained one crucial factor running throughout, and that was THE SEA. Considering it was only a few hundred yards from where I lived from baby age until fifteen, it was an important part of growing up.

I had an invisible mate, someone to whisper to and tell things. It could be devastatingly cruel during wintry gales, with its power to break or move whatever was in the way. It instigated lives being lost when fishing boats overturned and sank miles from land with loss of all crew members. Irrelevant of the size of any waterborne craft, the sea was master. It could not be beaten or tamed.

Broken sea walls, granite barrages, rusting bolts supporting weather-worn wood groynes are visible proof of its menacing strength. Nothing can prevent its encroachment upon ineffectual attempts to halt its breathtaking enormity. Today's scientists predict east-coast sea-bordering acreages from King's Lynn to parts of Essex will disappear in future decades, leaving immense swathes of emptiness relative to erosion and the strength of winds. It doesn't bear thinking about. Terrible thought!

There were times when I wandered out to the pier heads, head down against the screaming ice-cold wind, and had to turn round to stabilise standing up. The force of wind kept me upright but facing the wrong direction. It took my young breath away.

Another factor was, I never wore the correct clothing for going out in dire, bloody, awful weather. The cap I wore easily lifted off, and I got annoyed having to pick it up every few yards. Had wellington boots on, but they produced sores from chafing, being too large. I could not win!

Looking back all those years ago, we really did some stupid things. Like scrambling over slippery, slimy seaweed-encrusted boulders and rocks under the old extension pier heads, searching for crabs. The tide could easily have stranded us and, within a few minutes, would have drowned all trespassers. Silly young sods, without a doubt. They had no nerves when young!

Plus, if any of us slipped on the dangerous surfaces, heads would come second best against the impassive, mute, million-year-old, unloving, uncaring bedrock foundations.

In madcap summer months, playing in front of the coastguard hut, on the rocks, I clearly remember a really idiotic, stupid and dangerous fad was sitting on old bent tin trays (never knew where they came from), holding on for dear life, and mates threw sand beneath the trays, while someone else gave a hearty push and, in seconds, hurtled down parts of the old seawall at a speed unknown to us devil-may-care young nutters.

There were only a few occasions when someone fell off, which was lucky considering the number of rocks and large broken slabs of concrete jutting out, only inches from the speed-mad unthinking lads. The crazy things we did?!

English is Easy? Who Says?

(This is by an unknown lady poet, copied from a magazine.)

We begin with a fox. The plural is foxes.

The plural of ox is oxen, not oxes.

One fowl is a goose, more are called geese,

More than one moose are never called meese.

One may see a lone mouse or a nest full of mice,

Plural of house is houses, not hice.

If more than one man is referred to as men,

Surely more than one pan ought to be pen?

If I speak of a foot and how you show me two feet,

When I give you a book, would two be a beek?

If one is a tooth and several are teeth,

Really two booths should be called beeth.

If the singular is this and the plural is these,

When I give you a kiss, would you give me

Several kese?

You speak of a brother and also of brethren,

But though you say mother, you never say methren.

The masculine pronouns are he, his and him,

But imagine the feminine, she, shes and shim.

Oh yes, English is easy the way it is spoken,

But I'm having problems getting it proper wroten.

'It's a puppet' (Brian Connelly)

'I've arrived and to prove it, I'm here (Max Bygraves.) 1950s Radio.

'That's a good idea SON' also Max Bygraves.

A Desolate Country Church

In and around a country churchyard, it is not as empty as first seen.

A visiting frog has adventurous ideas of how and where to go to dream. Other

insects are busy and thriving, flitting to and from at play,

Searching, feeding, diving, enjoying every pleasant trouble-free day.

In quiet, warm summer evenings, gnats hang hovering near tall hedges.

On the leaves are caterpillars, sheltering under protective edges.

Seasons leave their calling cards as time rolls by, and winter attracts...

An owl on guard in dense dark forest persistently hunts for voles and rats.

Picturesque snow scenes, eye-wateringly vivid,

A solitary robin fills the air with song.

The silent churchyard sleeps on, regardless, but knows that New Year won't be

long.

If you visit any rural church, it will appear to be desolate (without onlookers),

yet living things so tiny you cannot observe their movements are there,

nonetheless, and exist without bother from any intruder.

My old imaginative mind is still 'fruitful' because the next few odes were

written from midnight until after one-thirty, November 2024.

Animal Anecdotes

Butterflies with wheezes, a dog with a cough,

A stick-insect sneezed and its left leg fell off.

A water hen with a phobia, a snake that loves to dance,

Two golden sheep from Bologna, a nest of mice from France.

A juggling duck with only one eye amazed his parents and mates,

Balancing mushrooms on his beak and smashing up large dinner plates.

A hedgehog rides a push-bike, wearing bright-coloured hats,

Had a terrible sight (he told me) and has run over a dozen cats.

When visiting a foreign country, a giraffe met a smiling panda,

They shared a meal of steak and veal,

Before falling off the fourth-floor veranda.

Goldfish and pilchards had a party,

Invited seals and snails.

An extrovert herring started singing

'Cos his father-in-law came from Wales.

An octopus playing bagpipes caused all sorts of troubles,

When someone asked for their favourite tune,

All they got were bubbles.

Two penguin mates from Devizes entered a fancy dress show.

Besides winning all the prizes, they were booked by a pantomime pro.

Gone but not Forgotten

This is in remembrance of a Ford Cortina Mark Three BAP 11K, in which my ex-wife and eldest daughter were in a 'freak accident' during a severe cold spell in December nineteen eighty-one. The recently resprayed, immaculate-looking car (with a new vinyl roof) spun on ice in front of the COOP canning factory, hit a concrete buffer on one side of the double doors, did a full circle by the impact, and hit the other buffer. The resulting damage wrecked the once-smart, cherished two-litre vehicle, which I sold as scrap for eighty-five pounds. I could have cried, did not take any photographs, either! The only good thing was no injuries, only bumps where two heads collided as they were thrown together.

When viewing a car that has been involved in an accident, it is shocking to see the amount of damage close up. Where you sat comfortably and enclosed from all exterior threats, looking through the windscreen, it is alien or dream-like, something surreal.

Casting an eye over the damage, it broke my emotional barrier to think that all life from the reliable motor had been stifled long before it was due. I stared at the malformed, crazily twisted wings, blue as a calm Mediterranean Sea. The shiny body lines, altered to a facsimile of sculpture, crumpled as though shaped by a hot candle or blowtorch. The polished, sparkling body that shone in hot summer suns and gleamed in cold wintry months slowly inhaled its final shallow breaths after experiencing the crash that caused its premature passing. Doors cannot shut properly due to the severity of the impact of metal and brickwork.

Wide, deep-etched scratches have penetrated layers of expertly sprayed paint. Chrome bumpers point skywards like a drunkard seeking truth, gazing at clouds. Headlights will never again pierce the darkness of night driving, although lamp glass is intact and peers squint-eyed at the pushed-in front metal grille. Even the steering wheel has changed to a more egg shape than before and will not accomplish any more well-executed three-point turns. The sad, unfortunate collision of car and solid wall has deformed metal under the engine; the sump is dented, and a hideous upturned grin resides. Lower suspension joints are bent askew, drag links cry at their new position of dangling freely from the safety of rubber bushes.

The streamlined, long, beautiful bonnet looks as though it has been crushed by two giant hands squeezing together and is shrivelled like a railway station sandwich turned up at the edges.

Straight lines of the regularly washed and groomed car are mere memories.

The car itself had died, but my memories live on, regardless. You will never be forgotten.

It might not be understood, writing an elegy for a car (or cars) you owned. But because of regular oil-changing, cleaning and maintaining each motor over the years, you become attached, therefore care, and look after it, don't you? As simple as that! The person I sold the car to (as scrap for £85) was a mechanic. Perhaps he brought it back to life and it had a decent second existence? I hope he did.

If I had my life over again, I would certainly have gone into car mechanics. In fact, I did a questionnaire about how an automobile runs and passed an introductory info sheet, but because I had mentioned the course, which was for two years commuting to Norwich, to a garage mechanic who at once replied, 'It's not recognised by our union,' and that put me off.

And did not enlist, I did regret that for ages, silly person indeed?

I always listened to what was being described and absorbed answers from those who were accustomed, qualified or in the industry, etc!

Whereas I should have ignored his advice and enrolled anyway.

An Option Sadly Chosen

Your door was slightly open. I heard the saddest crying.

I wanted to say 'I'm sorry,' although you would think I was prying.

Realising there's friction in relationships, arguments never resolved one iota.

With a thousand apologies on my lips, our marriage had reached its quota.

I made no noise as I walked away from a family home of thirteen years.

With tears in my eyes and pain in my heart,

From you, I would disappear.

The only poem relative to my divorce in 1986.

I wrote it after leaving my former matrimonial home with all my worldly goods in a black bin bag, after twenty-five years and two weeks of marriage. When true love is no longer existent, that is the time to make a break. And I did.

Did not want to make life more difficult money-wise for an ex-wife and two young daughters and relinquished my legal entitlement to 'half the house' value and started life on my own. Without a "pot to piss in", an old car my only thing of value, and in digs for the first time in my life.

(Thinking many months later, I should never have done such a caring act.)

Viewing Time

Beside a flickering candle bathed in its glow is a head

a few feet from a curtainless window, a creative person lays dead.

The bedroom is quite dark and cold

with a cupboard and rattan chair

on which a clock with a red digital dial

casts warmth to the dark head of hair.

All body life has sadly ceased,

no motion will recover again.

The silence is almost emotional,

light pattering on the window (the rain).

As the candle flickers steadily,

wax melts its journey down.

As living must proceed its path,

the face in the bed, not a frown.

This vivid recurring sombre sight

brings tears to a regretful theme.

After the candle has burnt itself out,

how long to reality, this dream?

Lifeline

I Watched a Television Documentary

And wanted to help those people that had been disruptively bombed. Richard Burton's magnificent narrative described the harshest severity as German troops invaded Holland. Flickering film showed dive-bombers, powerful land guns, sandy beaches, exploding shells and dotted fires. Bomb blasts, collapsed buildings, devastated towns, cities and obscene views of charred bodies being taken away in donkey and horse carts. (A cruel indication of what man could do against man.)

Honest peasant folk trying to make a meagre living from the land did not have a chance to protect themselves against well-organised, death-dealing methods of elimination from a man who would die from a disease he so aptly deserved. Yet, through hardship, pain, and seeing a lifetime's work ruined in front of their eyes, they gave thumbs-up gestures and weak smiles that showed their spirit would not flag under temporary invaders.

Through roaring sounds of war, screaming aeroplane engines, tanks and motorbikes, Burton's voice was Churchill's voice. NOTHING could elaborate such criminal events set to offend decency and common sense.

BUT I wanted to help as I watched a television documentary and felt saddened by the horrific things I had witnessed.

I always get inspiration after viewing documentaries.

Winter Rain

Stinging cold November rains,

wash pavements then vanish down drains,

splattering against double-glazing windowpanes.

Bends heavy flower-heads, hits drooping leaves,

slides down stalks without reprise.

Trickles, travelling down a plastic pipe, into barrels out of sight,

A garden sink with a rubber hose, slowly, so slowly, overflows.

Showers halt, remains a glistening cleaner face,

a prim and proper backyard space.

The pleasant damp smell of rich, pure soil,

while underneath, earthworms squirm and recoil.

Stinging cold November rains,

wash over pavements, then vanish down drains.

Splattering ceaselessly on the double-glazed windowpanes.

I use rainwater for my paintings.

Donald Whitmore

I met Donald Whitmore via an advertisement to do with writers and poetry. He was a tall, elderly, educated gentleman with a sister living in the same seafront hotel, opposite a popular pier with a fish and chip restaurant, skating rink and nightclub that welcomed jazz bands and evening cabaret guests.

He had a slight leaning-forward stance and by the time I left, fully knew the reason. Remarkably, he shared bus seats with the famous artist L. S. Lowry, creator of Matchstick Men. Both came from Salford. Donald had been a professional pianist and wrote music and poetry. I left him a small collection of my works to see what he thought.

Two weeks later, he invited me back and, thankfully, liked what I had written. He commented "You have great talent," and remarked, "You should read The Masters, follow the techniques, learn how phrases flow" which was great for my ego, but to read tomes of great writers dating back centuries was too time-consuming, plus I would get none of my writing done. He gave me a self-penned piece of prose written on an established, correct metre. I think of him whenever I read it. His background must have been associated with wealth because before moving to the coast, they (his sister with him) lived in a large country home with gardens, servants, a gardener, and a driver. Must have been a drastic event for them, but I never enquired. He spoke slowly in a bass-like tone. Before I left, he made me smile when mentioning, "If I stand on a chair, I can see the sea from the topmost window.

I was told of both their deaths many months later. I had met someone that knew Lowry. How good was that? Dear Donald Whitmore.

The Old Piano

A failure in life, a humble clerk,

he turned for respite to paintbrush and books,

but most of all, to his old piano, which vexed his uncomprehending wife.

He played not unskilfully, shed the load,

from the parlour outpouring, the while his wife

banged pots and pans together wilfully.

Then she would say, "Enough of that,

come down from the clouds, there's washing-up."

He heard and inwardly rebelled but could do no other than obey.

His wife's displeasure conquered him.

At length, he felt he could play no more.

In bitterness of soul, he thought,

"Let it suffice, I will sell my treasure."

And when he told her, pale and quiet,

that he planned to offer it for sale,

the old silk-lined instrument, she said,

"Good — 'twill help pay for our coal."

New Man on the Scene

(Surrealistic picture of human existence in a future world.)

Over the hills of solitude, across choking deserts of despair,

you turn first left and there it is, a place without compassion or care.

Ignore the hands of beggars, shuffle through crowds of dying!

Don't hesitate to heed the sick or frail... that noise? It is only crying.

Crying from hundreds of long-dead souls that never had wills of their own.

Their tortured brains burst with agony before they became full grown.

They never knew what happiness was, or joy, or trust, or hope.

They simply shrunk and passed away because they couldn't cope.

You do not have to stare at those babies' blue eyes

or pay attention to their starving plight,

abandoned children is a sickening craze, we put them in bins overnight.

Yes, those dogs seem hideously fat. Do you not know the reason?

Where have you been, new man on the scene?

Human flesh is always in season.

Do not weep at disfigured beings, it's cancer and leprosy,

there are no doctors nor medicines here,

by the way, are you stopping for tea?

An old saying, lost in the mists of time.

A woman is like an oven, must be warmed up before meat is inserted!

Under the Old Oak Tree

Adjoining land belonging to farmer George Mann, contractors were brought in to remove an obstacle in Harpers Lane, a two-hundred-year-old trunk of an oak tree. Not until a fatal accident involving a young labourer being crushed against its bulk had anything been done to remove it from the well-used country lane.

Two days passed. A hole around the tree had been dug. Thick roots were open to the November Norfolk air. By the size of the trunk, it must have been a giant amongst trees. Everything progressed nicely until something was found wedged between smaller roots. It looked like a wooden sea chest. Because the object was whole and undisturbed, the site work supervisor, in a rare moment of wisdom and foresight, said it might be a treasure trove. With this firmly planted in his mind, he got in touch with someone that knew someone who worked in Norwich Castle Museum, who instructed them to cease work immediately.

A bearded man accompanied by a petite female assistant took lots of measurements, chatted continuously until a police car arrived. The copper took out four metal spikes and a long length of red and white plastic tape and set about encircling the tree to keep the public away. As if tape would prevent people from staying away?

Monday arrived, and two workers nailed notices to the object of interest. An official document stated it was part of a historic dig. Local photographers came to peer into the excavated ground to view the squatter and a group of villagers stood talking by a gateway to the field. One person in a group of elderly men was heard to say, "At moight be one a' them bombs they dropped durin' the war, yew dunt know dew yer?"

Nothing and nobody were seen for several days until council workers, armed with chainsaws, selected and rapidly sawed through enough roots to attempt to dislodge the mystery item. Farm workers helped by council workers snipped through clinging roots holding the chest-like item, tidied branches and foliage, ready for a good old bonfire, which would be nice to feel heat in the near-freezing atmosphere. An anticlimax — the box was not heavy at all, although it looked cumbersome. Taken away without fuss or bother to a department within the Castle Museum, nothing came to light till after New Year, when an official-looking headed envelope was handed in at the farm receptionist's office.

Meanwhile, the bulk of the tree had been systematically trimmed of all branches before a tractor tugged, heaved and finally withdrew the trunk from its birthplace with only the hole as witness to the occasion.

It was set fire to (eventually) and interested villagers cast a glimpse at the roaring, crackling, welcoming heat, with a fire crew standing by for any emergency.

In the warmth of his office, the farm manager opened the document and read out its contents to his farm staff, with details of what had been done to the tree. He began by describing how it had been sprayed, scraped, X-rayed and solvents applied to diagnose whatever they had found. It was just an old metal box but had layers of a tar-like substance covering its entire surface. It was in good condition but had not been dated.

The letter began, 'it was not treasure trove', which was the main thing the farm workers wanted. But there may be future digs because the assistant said, 'there are other aspects to do with what was in the box that need looking into', but gave no indication of what they might be. The farm workers smiled to one another in mild excitement.

There were loads of technical wordings, scientific facts and three drawings before coming to the last explanation of what had been deposited in the box.

1. A rough-textured jacket/jerkin with leather thongs
2. A quantity of woven material, sheepskin
3. Two earthenware jugs or pots
4. Several leather pouches, one contained dog's teeth
5. Lots of tiny sharp flints
6. A crumpled bundle of sackcloth
7. The last item shocked them all.
8. Wrapped in the sackcloth... was...
9. A young human child's body.

This was related to my grandfather by an even older gentleman that bartered rabbits for straw and flowers for eggs, which was a common practice years ago. Not sure if it was one of those country myths?

As a Small Kid in Short Trousers

I had to go to a backyard which was next door to a butcher's shop to collect, of all things, BLOOD, which was added copiously to grandfather's roses. The bloke filled the bucket and, trying to keep upright, walking in a straight line, my clothes and legs were splashed with dribbles that escaped over the brim of the bucket. Good job mother never saw me, or it would have warranted a slap or a flick round the ears.

I was never lonely as a kid because I would go with grandfather whenever he wanted me, and his mates would ask me to help with small jobs from which they gave me 'threepence' or two humbugs or a chewing gum. I loved chopping up sticks for fires. Collecting fresh lavender always caused me to sneeze up to six times, one after the other. The ladies of the houses made tiny bags of loose lavender for their cupboards to keep moths away. No wonder their clothes smelt.

One very old lady neighbour, Mrs Patterson, often sat in her back garden, which contained apple trees. I would peek over grandfather's fence to see if she was there and if not, would hurriedly nip in through her rear gate entrance and shovel up as many of the fallen crop as possible. This backfired on me because if she called over and wanted me to do shopping, she would reward me by giving a bowl of apples, it was all great fun. I willingly scoffed them!

On separate occasions, mother and grandmother told me a fact which now, as an old man, gives me the wobbles with a slight nauseous feeling. I would wander through the enormous allotment containing every fruit and vegetable and pick off and eat whatever I fancied and then sit behind the small greenhouse in which grew the most wonderful plump tomatoes.

They remarked that if everything went quiet, apparently, I was forever singing or making humming noises, they knew what I was doing next comes the horrible reality image: sitting on the ground, legs splayed, in my one-piece fluffy jumpsuit, with slime and snot around face and chin.... chewing... snails… How in heaven's name could ANYONE do such a thing? It does not bear thinking about.

'Goodnight children, everywhere' (Uncle Mac) BBC Radio Children's Programme during the late 1940s/1950s.

A couple of feet from their back door and kitchen at grandparents' house was an underground well from which fresh water was hauled up in a bucket. This, to my enquiring mind, was magic. I would peer down into the water and wait for ages to see if any fish might appear (such was my thinking). The water was ice-cold even in summer and must have been essential for many purposes throughout their life. I was spellbound, simply looking into the darkened watery space. It fascinated me.

Grandmother used the water for shampooing her hair. Never knew if the outlet was filled in and did not think about it while on that TV visit.

And a traditional metal shoe/boot scraper stood on passive guard at the back door!

Conscience Re-Revisited

In younger days, time was comfortably absent, no immediate rush except to accomplish nasty, inconsiderate, spiteful acts on defenceless living insects, like picking off wings from flies that circled overhead. Thought it was fun to do such things... it doesn't matter anymore, or does it?

Catching slow-moving earthworms sniffing the cool fresh air from a break of their darkened existence, I cut them into tiny slices with a knife grandfather owned to amuse myself, watching the segments wriggle, squirm and do twisting dances. I was amazed they were alive; it does not matter anymore, or does it?

Threw bottles with tops on into the mirror-like water of a ship dock. Grabbed a chunk of chalk from a wall and threw it at the bottle that nonchalantly bobbed and dipped as if ridiculing my aim. Laughed as a hit cracked the bottle, which slowly sank out of sight into debris-strewn depths of my childhood playground. It does not matter anymore, or does it?

In hot summer months, I searched for insects and, using a magnifying glass, would focus the prism, burn the victim until smoke and a smell of burning showed how good the glass was. It does not matter anymore, or does it?

When mother said, 'Don't go far, tea is nearly ready', I walked as far as I could before turning back, then ambled into the humble household without a thought of what she had prepared in the frugal existence she ran. I never thought how difficult it must have been looking after two kids on her own.

I did not care!

Chased cats and dogs for devilment and if I caught one, tugged its tail trying to pull it off or, with help from a bucket of water, flick and splash them to get them angrier or stare them out. Gran had a cocker spaniel, Nellie, which lived in a large handmade kennel beneath a tall evergreen bush. I cuddled her lots and could fit in the kennel.

A family friend introduced me to a young ginger-haired girl with plaits and sticking-out teeth. Was told to show her flowers grandfather grew in his garden. The girl pulled my hair, I bit one of her fingers, she cried. I laughed! It matters no more, or does it? Looking back to those mischievous, hurtful acts, I must have been a right little bugger without feelings for each event or creature. Did not think about it or was sorry. Years later, those actions embarrass me because I am a sincere, thoughtful, caring person, love animals and appreciate nature. It is a conscience thing.

I am apologising for those senseless incidents. It does matter, you know.

I hope most sincerely, dear reader, you have enjoyed the re-captured mixed contents. You may have heard some of the sayings or forgotten most, but my wish was to retain them for the future because times and opinions change rapidly. One generation might thoroughly enjoy the obscurity, whereas current mindsets may consider them totally rubbish and bland, there you go? Cannot please all the people all the time. I tried at least! Words cannot make an object solid but certainly assist structure and layout of an idea.

I have alternative examples of creativity but ideally, my effort and the power of words will identify my ambition as something different. I hope so. The pencil of my master plan has only one inch remaining. I haven't ordered any more!

I opened the door and IN-FLU-ENZA.

I would not say she was ugly but her toothpaste refused to come out of the tube.

A celebrity works hard to become well known then wears dark glasses to not be recognised. (Fred Allen)

Have no fear towards perfection, you will never reach it. (Salvador Dali)

Opera is when a guy gets stabbed in the back and instead of bleeding... he sings. (Ed Gardner)

All music is folk music. Never seen an animal singing. (Louis Armstrong)

They couldn't find the artist... so they hung the painting. (Gerald F. Lieberman)

Must go now. I am having an old friend for dinner. (From *Silence of the Lambs*)

Give an inch to a woman, she thinks she is a ruler. (Anon)

Have been asked to write my life story, can anyone remember what I was doing between 2000–2012? Thanks.

My wife is a light eater as soon as it's light, she eats. (Henry Youngman)

Calamari custard with small beetroots on the side,

honeyed wasps laid out around each platter,

after several vodka tonics, it will not seem that bit chronic,

eat up, enjoy it because it does not really matter.

Foreign food has taken over English traditional grub.

Fish, roast beef and cauliflower have all been given the snub.

Unusual food is on display in restaurants and hotels.

Strange-sounding names with spices and pungent meaty smells.

Packets of deep-fried flying things, mosquitoes marinated with gins.

Served with heaps of French fries. Dessert is maggots in tins, aniseed mashed potatoes,

mustard-flavoured crisps.

Beware the homemade Vindaloo bread, it is bound to burn your lips.

Six slick skipping Suffolk sheep were sheltering from rain.

Susan, the eldest of the clan, shouted out…

sod this… we will catch a train.

I take my children everywhere, but they always find their way back home. (Robert Orben)

Youth is such a wonderful thing, shame it is wasted on children. (George Bernard Shaw)

There are hundreds of quotations I perused but thought better of it. I wanted to be original. With other people's work, I would not have achieved that!

"Nice to see you…. to see you…. nice." (Bruce Forsyth)

Beach View at Daybreak

How can this disguise I see be the same death-bringing stormy winter-freezing weather? A false veneer bears no semblance to an angry, menacing roaring enormity I watched as a young boy when it drenched me, chilled my innocent frail frame to the bone, and when I got home, mother was peeved because my clothes were wet from standing too close to the frothing, splashing water; bordering the area that was my playground as a child, the beach area where I had lived from baby age until fifteen years old.

From where I stood, admiring the shimmering, calm, early morning North Sea, the image gave no evidence of the cruelty it could appoint with terrible fierceness and magnitude no other element could be capable of!

A pack of lies. Gazing into slow-approaching, gentle-lapping wavelets, the sun suddenly pierced the orange-yellow streaked clouds of dawn.

The ominous, magnificent power is sleeping contentedly (perhaps) for a while. Kindly do not disturb. You do not want to see it angry?

Modern-day planning has limited the amount of sand to the children's corner by barrages created from huge marble boulders. It is not frequented in the way it was, and tides prevent spaces for deckchairs or shallow water paddling.

Female Allure

From Egyptian treasures in pyramids found,

thousands of years undiscovered underground.

Montezuma's great Mexican splendour, natural beauty cannot surrender,

to a magnificent feminine display on view, without being locked away.

Female allure, its bodily enticement,

nothing as satisfying, crammed with excitement.

Emeralds, diamonds, pearls, gold,

nothing compares to caress and hold.

The female body with accessories built-in,

far more intoxicating than vodka or gin.

Perfumed, powdered, made-up, kissable.

Nothing BUT NOTHING is so irresistible.

But attempting to nurture an instinctive need,

that varies a diet to physically feed,

an innermost secretive, desirous prize,

that creates temptations with just a look in the eyes.

Beauty is more than a makeover weekend,

from initial introduction to more than a friend.

There is no comparison to female allure.

A biased statement? Of course, of that, I am sure.

A young chef had passed exams for a qualification with one final interview to do. If successful, he could work in the best hotels. He had to demonstrate to a seated committee of experts how good he was and chose eggs as his topic.

On stage, dressed in immaculate cooks' whites (without a pointy hat), he bowed to the faces looking up at him and went through his routine.

First, spun six eggs on the tabletop for a few seconds, which was marvellous to witness… picked them up… juggled like a circus performer… expertly rolled them around his neck and shoulders… for a few seconds… did the juggling again before finally cracking them at record speed into a Pyrex jug. There was no response from the dour-faced examiners.

The head of the committee stood up and went over to the young man.

'How did I do? Have I passed?' asked the hopeful young chef.

The man replied, "Sorry, NO… you piss about too much."

If her brain had a race with his brain... they would be two non-runners.

The four most important words in a marriage: "I'll do the dishes."

2 YY's UR... 2 YY's UB... 1CUR... 2 YY's... 4ME (Have to think hard?)

Jock stood on the burning deck. Snowy rang the hooter... who do you think came round the bend? Dick Barton on a scooter. (For old readers)

Two little dickybirds sitting on a wall, one named Peter, the other named Paul.

Fly away Peter, fly away Paul, come back Peter... come back Paul.

Witness to an accident… By Willy B. OK?

Man in constant agony… By Claude Balls

Ladies' favourite… By Ivor Big'un.

Children Sing-Songs at School

The farmer wants a wife, the farmer wants a wife, Ei Annie oh, the farmer wants a wife.

The wife wants a child, the wife wants a child,

Ei Annie oh, the wife wants a child.

The child wants a dog, the child wants a dog, Ei Annie oh... the child wants a dog.

We all pat the dog; we all pat the dog. Ei Annie oh.... we all pat the dog.

(This was an infants' school rhyme.)

Patter cake, patter cake, baker's man,

bake me a cake as fast as you can.

Pat it and prick it and mark it with a B,

put it in the oven for baby and me.

One potato, two potato, three potato, four,

five potato, six potato, seven potato, more.

And OUT spells out!

Suffolk

Flat as far as an eye can see, Constable landscape, empty, free.

Sheep with cattle, donkey, or horses,

abide their time beside watery courses.

Abundant fish in clear deep rivers,

willows, reeds in cool breeze shivers.

Dykes and bridges, weirs, and moats,

commercial holidays in meandering boats.

Partridge, coot, swan and pheasant,

add to something more than pleasant.

Heron on guard during summer evenings' lull,

different in winter, flocks of herring gull.

Otters chase one another around,

while tiny water vole escapes the sound

of calling duck, swan and bittern,

this wonderful Suffolk,

in our beloved Great Britain.

Nostalgia is not what it used to be.

'Hello, playmates.' (Arthur Askey, radio broadcaster and TV.)

'Take my mother-in-law, PLEASE!' A popular phrase.

A Way of Life

Trees grow wonderfully tall and straight, reaching to the sky,

but the way we humans grow old and fade sometimes makes us cry.

Although the mind still functions, reactions tend to slow down,

aches in arms, legs and hips, hair disappears from the crown.

Eyes cannot focus as when we were young, clearly saw the way

across summer meadows with grasses, flowers and hay.

We jumped and hopped, laughed a lot, fell on our knees and cried,

wanted to kiss every girl in the class; some boys had tried.

Wished for Christmas presents that parents couldn't buy,

and hated when we got some socks, an orange or a tie.

Youth became the time of life when crimes might turn our heads

to clearer thoughts of school and leaving, common sense instead.

Some did things they wanted to, like driving a car or a bus,

others stayed miserably at home with mum and made a fuss.

Some completed chosen employments, stayed until retirement.

I experienced many significant tasks; that was my requirement.

Funeral of Diana, Princess of Wales

(Written while watching the television broadcast.)

Silence, oh, the enveloping silence, overwhelming, emotional.

Only horses' hooves, clicking of brass against leather,

soldiers' precise marching boots on tarmac,

every minute one muffled bell,

accompanied a gun-carriage coffin

on a bright, sunlit public occasion.

White tulips and lilies placed on top of the Royal Coat of Arms,

never realised how the world would focus on their simplicity.

How many tears fell from public and private eyes

during that monumental procession through London streets

that showed unimaginable respect

towards an individual who also showed

great respect and compassion and love

to those of lesser upbringing?

A sadder moment in history never existed.

It was an emotional, almost surreal occasion watching the cortege,

witnessing a public funeral that was silent. It was unique.

Sunset, Acle, Norfolk

October sky, an upside-down version of sunrise,

colour schemes of orange, red-mauve, purple,

slowly streak across the heavens, then lazily drift down,

gradually sinking into the countryside, as evening clouds approach with marshmallow

enormity,

to kiss, merge and completely engulf the heron haven, kestrel kingdom.

As daylight disappears, reed-bowing breezes expire,

and a sense of suspended wonder exists — albeit briefly.

How many upside-down sunrises my sentimental eyes witness,

such wonderful, beautiful, natural, unforgettable sights?

Looking left to right, distance and behind,

the low-lying vastness until tomorrow's neglected sunrise

reappears to display its exhibitionistic, splendid

presentation many people take for granted,

but leaves observers enchanted by its ever-changing

brightness of colour, bathing every flower, caressing every hour,

playing visionary tricks of picturesque beauty.

No music could accompany its presence, nor singer sing its praise.

If the upside-down sunrise transpires,

we'll have the most enjoyable of days.

The man's loving hands touched the face as if to trace

every delightful inch with delicate fondness.

A playful, gentle finger wanted to loiter, linger,

and caress neat eyebrows, reaching down past cascading crown.

The hands came to rest upon sloping neck and breast.

Breathing and heart rate began to race;

nervous sweat trickled from temple and face.

But unblinking, unresponsive eyes

looked blankly through him to distant skies.

He wanted to experience the inviting lips

before pleasure gave measure to total eclipse.

It might cause distaste, horror or disgust

to see an old, bearded sculptor

kiss an angelic marbled bust.

The Sculptor

There Never Seems Enough

There never seems enough weeks in the year or hours in a day

There never seems enough seconds in the hour

or enough money in your pay

There never seems enough compassion about or assistance it seems

There never seems enough sincerity

or enjoyment in our dreams

There always seems too much bargaining,

never a factual release

There is never a true meaning of hope,

never a sign of peace

There never seems enough time to survive

or aims towards better living

There never exists true awareness,

or an improved way of giving

There never seems enough time to laugh

yet plenty it seems for crying

There seldom seems enough gratitude

but sufficient bodies are trying

A... TO... Z

Birth...living....to venture through life

Learn expert knowledge.... span your thoughts

Experience everything available,

and die with contented ambitions.

Climb over a rainbow,

spray-paint a passing cloud

try shaking hands with a lobster

at midnight shout out LOUD.

How Much?

How much money in this world? How much mortar to build?

How many people are suffering? How many injured or killed?

How many ways of evil? How much the wages of sin?

How much the price of freedom? How will we ever win?

How many stars in the heavens?

How many moons in the skies?

How much time have we got left?

How long the final sunrise?

How far the outer space, the beyond?

How narrow the innermost mind?

How can we get rid of disease?

How to cure the blind?

How can we help one another?

How to get shut of fears?

How far to go for happiness?

How long the coming years?

After That What Happens?

When you have waved goodbye to friends,

tied together two loose ends

filled up those old ink-type pens, after that what happens?

Blown out the smallest candlelight,

awakened in the morning from the night

coloured something dark before was bright,

after that, what happens?

Seen a cheerful, smiling face, laid another dinner place

spread an intricate shawl of lace

after that, what happens?

Displayed beautiful bouquets of scented flowers

watched a river for hours and hours. Admired those lofty old-world towers

after that, what happens?

Suffered from an experience, laughed and cried

felt terrible when somebody close had died

at least for you told truths seldom lied

after that, what happens?

Built items of interest with your hands

surveyed people from distant far lands

viewed tides which covered dangerous sands. After that, what happens?

Not For Me

Never heard voices that told me to kill

didn't need drugs for an unfulfilled thrill

or was easily persuaded to burgle and steal

drinking before sitting behind a car's steering wheel

Inner-most thoughts were an incoming tide

shallow yet always many miles wide

Never bothered by rain pouring down

hopefully, intentionally never wore a frown

Seldom bothered by thunderstorm's power,

wants and wishes slowly climbed a tall tower......

whose steps were slippery from previous aims

(never ever good at athletic games)

Fridays played football at boring left-back

forever failing on a fast-running track

Appreciated conversation, meals with red wine

when smiles and laughter made loneliness shine.

Numerous yearnings were blown by a breeze

scattering like autumnal leaf-dropping trees

never envious, jealous or yearned for wealth

throughout my existence was aware of my health.

Never abused, misused, took things for granted

seeds of selfishness were never planted

Discovered ambitions in life go astray

but clearly remain in my mind to this day.

The Fox and Salmon Inn

Not too far from a rural market town is a first-class eatery,

tastefully redecorated with colour co-ordinated tints

no harsh vulgar maroons, dreary beige, custard-yellow

walls or facsimile plastic ornaments.

Seating is made from genuine wooden beer barrels.

Large cushions make comfortable the hard, shiny, slippery surfaces

resulting from backsides sitting on them over the years.

Unobtrusive guitar music plays in the background.

A pleasant riverside modernised inn with good selective menus,

a well-stocked wine cellar and young, pleasant, smiling staff.

A countryside residence off the road

where brash, noisy chewing-gum townies go

for rump steak, garlic mushrooms,

French fries, onion rings with side salad.

And outside in spacious echoing,

water-running immaculate toilets,

spit, spew, and piss

on a sixteenth-century floor.

Can't Swallow That

An environmental thought for the future.

Please don't tread on the marshmallow carpet

or shake the pear-drop flowers

don't eat those lemonade petals,

you'll have stomach-ache for hours

Can you risk touching that enormous peppermint tree?

There's danger in dried bananas.

You will have to remove your shoes

and socks when walking on hills of sultanas.

Add water to sherbet bread and wait until the froth dies down

then it's safe to eat but watch your tongue turn slowly brown.

Hot soya meat pies and fish and chips are sold in machines over there; octopus is this

month's preference and so is yellow hair.

Curried wasps and Mornay prawns are this week's special price

as well as honeyed frogs' legs, they're really very nice.

Beef and lamb and pork and veal are illegal foodstuffs now,

there's a shortage of pigs and sheep and cow.

Chicken, rabbit, pheasant and duck are taxable; trout is great,

oranges, apples are cheap as chips; you buy them by the crate.

Sweets are banned by legislation.

A thriving black market for chocolate and toffee,

small game birds are for take-away meals.

There's a worldwide embargo on coffee.

Ketchup and saucers have been replaced by relish margarines

which are composite spreads of flavourings

that you add to potatoes and greens.

Sugar is sold in liquid form, replacing bags that split,

sausages are made from peanuts and barbecued on a spit.

Cordon Bleu, haute cuisine is only seen in classes

of catering establishments

that supply wine in long-stemmed glasses.

Never-Ending...

Steel. Zinc. Copper. Iron.

Tiger. Leopard. Panther. Lion.

Stars. Moon. Planets. Sun. Whistle. Sing. Lah-Lah. Hum.

Path. Road. Avenue. Street. Arms. Legs. Hands. Feet.

Peach. Plum. Apricot. Pear. Nose. Eye. Head. Hair.

Ocean. Sea. River. Stream. Dull. Sparkle. Glitter. Gleam.

Distant. Close. Far. Yonder. Kawasaki.

Yamaha. Suzuki. Honda.

Fish. Bird. Animal. Poultry.

Peppery. Vinegary. Mustardy. Salty.

Pen. Pencil. Crayon. Chalk.

Run. Trot. Jog. Walk.

Dog. Cat. Budgie. Canary.

Elf. Gnome. Witch. Fairy.

Green. Black. Purple. Blue.

Skirt. Jumper. Socks. Shoe.

Rain. Frost. Thunder. Snow.

Catch. Carry. Fling. Throw.

Box. Tin. Bag. Sack.

Hit. Whip. Kick. Smack.

Cup. Saucer. Teapot. Tray.

September. June. March. May.

Cricket. Football. Rugby. Bowls.

Squirrels. Badgers. Fox. Moles.

A first school tune when using a double skipping rope.

Sing a song of sixpence a pocket full of rye

four and twenty blackbirds baked in a pie

when the pie was opened, the birds began to sing

wasn't that a dainty dish to set before the King?

The King was in the counting house, counting out his money

The Queen was in the parlour eating bread and honey.

The maid was in the garden hanging out her clothes

when down came a blackbird and pecked off her nose.

Another similar dance-to tune was

Daisy Daisy, give me your answer do,

I'm half crazy all for the love of you.

It won't be a stylish marriage, I cannot afford a carriage,

but you'll look sweet upon a seat of a bicycle made for two.

Jack Spratt could eat no fat, his wife could eat no lean

so between them both, you see, they licked the platter clean.

Today will be yesterday tomorrow.

Why?

A head-bent saddened mother sat beside a hospital bed

of her teenaged, comatose, pale-faced son, remembering words he had said. "I'm

sorry, Mum," tearfully he told her, "What a bloody fool I've been."

Now she recalls him growing up, his normality she had seen.

Happy times they all had shared, his sister, dad and a cat

with boyish grin, laughing eyes and his home-made cricket bat.

The day he fell out of his pushchair was the time he broke his nose,

those terrible noisy records he bought, those awful teenage clothes.

One evening he came home soaked through. Mates were having a lark.

Months later the truth came out, he'd fallen into the lake in the park.

"I'd had a few drinks, Mum," he admitted. She took it as a fact without prying.

Looking back, it was the first occasion of his change, she started crying.

The darkened days and empty nights waiting for a ring of the 'phone,

hearing her son, "Hello Mum, everything's okay but I'm not coming home."

What had she done, had tried her best at being a caring mother?

(now a comatose, pale, haggard druggie). Perhaps he wanted a brother?

He'd forsaken her and his family, disregarded love and compassion,

security and a comfortable home, he lived only for his ration,

of injections, pills and shivering thrills, throwing up and filthy dirty.

The heart-broken, questioning mother asked WHY?

To her dying youngest child, AGED ONLY THIRTY.

This is the SADDEST EVER recollection, when I was not ready for life's challenges and relive this heart-breaking experience with explosive clarity. On an early shift in the airmen's mess at Marham, had a telephone call from a woman attending my wife (about to go into labour) who advised me to "come home immediately, there's an emergency."

Those fifteen miles from camp via Swaffham to Holme Hale were a speeding blur. I couldn't think straight. What on earth had happened? Hell to the speed limit! No one was waiting for me at the rear door of the country cottage but as I entered, a female voice called down, "Up here." I could hear crying as I leapt up the steep creaking staircase, three steps at a time.

I cannot recall if the woman was a nurse or medical officer of some sort; she beckoned me over. Margaret was sobbing uncontrollably in the other bedroom. "Help me," she pointed to a plastic bag on the bed. "He wouldn't have suffered," and indicated I place the bag into a box while she held open the lid. Shock of shocks. I briefly handled the bag containing my fully formed stillborn baby boy's body as it flopped into the cardboard box, to which the woman folded over the lids and said, "that's for the mortuary surgeon," and beckoned, "go see your wife." A dreadful thing to have experienced at such an age? I WAS 18 YEARS OLD.

If anybody claims to have gone through a trauma, I can substantiate what happened to me that day is by far the most upsetting and never-to-be-forgotten single sad event to experience, especially at such a young age. I recall every detail!

From 2006, I made enquiries to agencies relevant to stillbirths, including Thames Valley Police Coroner's Office, child-bereavement studies gave their advice, ending with SANDS (Stillbirth and Neonatal Death Society). The staff were brilliant. They sent a stillbirth certificate with the cause of his death. November 20th 1961, subarachnoid haemorrhage, which usually occurs during birth! He is buried unnamed in an unmarked grave in Marham village churchyard.

Snetterton

Snetterton in Norfolk was the nearest motorcycle and racing car circuit, where I witnessed fantastic racing of bikes and drag cars, including past masters of each. I had sold souvenir programmes bought in the early seventies but wish I had not (as you do). Names like Barry Sheene, Phil Read, Bill Ivy, Mike Hailwood (who celebrated his twenty-first birthday wearing a white overall on top of his racing leathers, riding an MV Agusta) also sidecar events. Pip Harris, Chris Vincent, Florian Camathias, Saw John Hobbs, Henk Vink, George Brown with both his Vincent monsters Nero I and II and other once-great record breakers, which I cannot recall (hence regret selling those programmes) at drag meetings. Alf Hagon too.

It was something else to see, hear and smell retro speed machines trying to go faster than other competitors. Each ear-splitting exhaust note made you screw your eyes up, and increased heart rate made it an occasion worth remembering. Seeing frail-looking 50 cc German bikes close-up made questions in the mind of "how the hell do they go so fast for something so small?" It is wonderful, the craftsmanship that goes into tuning engines, working out gear ratios, carburettor adjustments, tyre pressures, oil pressures ad infinitum, for minuscule, incredibly fast, screeching mini racing bikes. There were Triumphs with twin engines side by side. Home-made, home-tuned BSA-framed Nortons; two-stroke high-revving, screeching Japanese bikes (threatening British makes). It was exciting, memorable.

Even when rain postponed racing, you walked around admiring the machines brought from all over Britain. Motorcycle racing was and is still a global phenomenon. It bridges age and sex. Lady entrants briefly intruded into a masculine domain. Beryl Braine, on her tiny screaming tiddler, did Isle of Man and circuit racing, but to be honest, I am not au fait with current facts and figures.

My motorcycling days were interesting enough. Would have loved to own an Ariel Leader with weather protection or its sister sports Arrow with racing fairing. Or a Triumph Twenty-One. One of my ex-brothers-in-law owned a gleaming, huge-engine, pale green Sunbeam S8 which was attached to a twin adult sidecar. Besides having an electric starter, it featured a deep car-like sump and sounded different from motorcycles of the era. Was shaft-driven, something new in fact. Wonder where that ended up? Scott Squirrels were odd-looking. Had a distinctive sound of their own. Police ran almost-silent-running grey-painted Velocette Viceroy specials and heads spun round when a Viper or Venom started up. Glorious.

I will cease the romantic visionary idealism of memory. This was before Japan monopolised the market with high-revving, fast, multi-cylinder bikes with off-the-gauge speeds. Speed frightened me! The USA always had huge fans buying their prestigious Harley-Davidsons. I sat on one in the Olympia Motorcycle Show. It had a foot clutch, wonderful seating, balloon tyres and a sprung handlebar. Heh dilly do.

When a kid, one misjudged "good turn" could have been disastrous.

Ambling over dried grass and weeds of the pickling plots (years before Birds Eye came along) little me came upon a solid ball-shaped mass which I thought might help keep the meagre fire alight. First rolling it with my feet, it was too heavy to carry. The fire was already heaped with fine coal dust and a glow showed it was smouldering. As carefully as I could handle the stuff, got it into position, dead centre on top of the fire and left it. Only got as far as crossing the road before a man ran towards me pointing to our house, yelling, "Your mother will bloody kill you. What have you done?" Dense black smoke bellowed out through the open front door, spirals curled upwards from the chimney. It looked bad. Crowds appeared as if by invisible strings.

Never knew what the mysterious lump was until being told it could have exploded and set fire to our home. The composite mixture of diesel fuel and extracted oil was from bilges of tanker ships when they cleaned pipes before berthing ashore. How was I to know? I thought I was helping!

Two neighbours helped remove the dreaded lump which had started to melt. A strong odour of fuel oil remained for days. I selected only bits of wood from that day onwards.

I didn't bother to learn how to swim until in the RAF, where swimming was part of several choices within the large gymnasium, pool and training areas.

Nobody was left out because it was compulsory to attain a certain fitness regime. There were no excuses and, in the rare opportunity of attempting one, your chances of getting away with it were bloody impossible.

"Swimmers go to the head of the pool, others stay here," came from a thin instructor who was trying to grow a moustache. Most entrants could swim. He had a grand style of teaching and those first couple of hours will forever be locked away in my mind's eye. Lined us up, arm's-length span between each body, facing the shallow end. He then said, "I want you to be hundred-yard sprinters and get into starting blocks." This was odd. "I will be behind you one by one and touch you with this stick (which instantly appeared somehow). When you feel the prod, lean forward. You will automatically fall into the water." And we did. That was the first lesson of getting used to water over our heads. Nothing complicated there. Floating, surprisingly, was an early safety measure and remarkably quick to achieve.

A few lads couldn't do it to save their lives, with lots of spluttering, spitting out water and being silly beggars. It was dream-like, non-real to be in an alien environment but enjoying the moment. I wanted to dive under the water for an unexplained reason. But we slowly had to go back and forth across the shallow end attempting to do whatever swimming stroke we fancied. I didn't think about it and settled for the breaststroke, seemed easier to me! Most did the overarm, and six older chaps did the butterfly which was complicated and required more effort. Yet one more small but progressive element in the basic training of boy entrants that would last throughout our lives. I never looked back and found that swimming assisted my breathing, considering I had a lung condition.

I did have niggling worries prior to the initial medical examinations that I might not pass the standard required, but nothing was discovered!

Seven years later, in sweltering hot Libya, in cooling water of Tobruk harbour, I accomplished a momentous feat of swimming out from the safety of the rocks, where a group of us dived from, to venture halfway towards a huge berthed oil tanker, where waves halted further progress. This was not the kind of thing someone that didn't swim regularly should have been doing.

Shows how bloody daft I was, aged twenty-two!

The most productive, hard-worked, strenuous job was labouring in a gang of five landscape gardeners. Other employments had no finished product. This changed enormously and was surely the most satisfying of many and varied jobs I pursued, without a doubt! But at a cost!

This meant travelling to neighbouring counties as far as Hertfordshire, mainly because each contract paid an improved rate and had to stay from Monday to Friday in hotels.

Hence the better pay!

I was like a fish out of water, middle-aged, recently re-married and in a world of change, both physically and mentally. Had to work in the rain, ignoring the seeping cold water dripping down your neck. Treading in clay-bound topsoil, skidding while digging holes for dogwood saplings, working on an upward incline adding dozens of ground-covering plants or flattening turf from an enormous heap of potential lawn greenery. It was on the go from arrival, but having one hour break for lunch was most welcoming; although we walked into more than one supermarket, work clothes attired, mud on faces and shit-laden footwear. I felt uncomfortable and thought that any minute a manager or store security person would approach us and be told to leave, being so scruffy. But it never happened.

I had a repetitive, dirty, and smelly job involving creosote-covered fence panels, cant rails, and fence posts. A few years back, this would have caused great annoyance by perpetually sneezing, luckily not apparent!

But it was hard graft, sweating beyond comfort and hands hardened by the actual effort with each demanding requirement.

One early morning into the outskirts of Cambridge saw us trying our hardest to de-root longer trailing roots from a taller-than-usual mature tree being planted into a deep, wide hole beside a main road. We had an audience of nearby office workers who waved and blew kisses while we pushed, pulled, heaved and toiled against the underestimated oversized tree; at least it made some people's mundane work that bit more entertaining!

The tree would be in full bloom by now as well as a mature upright specimen.

Another city visit was north of Norwich on the Cromer Road, had a most surprising day's work in front of a Tesco store. Removing an unbelievable number of millions-of-years-old flint from within its resting place, for heavens only know what time factor. Great shapes, sharp edges, smooth areas and pointy bits had to be eased onto the small Mitsubishi open-back truck. I was amazed the quantity we removed would have overburdened the little motor, but it didn't, thankfully.

Some of the smaller flints still smile from my rear garden and make a comparison of shape, size and colour from other delightful blooms within the twenty-foot-long and twelve-foot-wide presentation.

The cost I mentioned. Working on a brand-new commercial site near Ely, suffered a lung collapse and had to relinquish the employment. I was gutted! The guys thought I had a heart attack.

It was as if a cold metal band had curled itself round my chest. I couldn't breathe properly. Was taken to the nearest doctor's surgery to have an intravenous injection and several inhalations of oxygen from a canister. Bloody hell!

Into the Millennium

The second visit to the hospital was for a hernia. Can't recall its name but was on my right-hand-side lower abdomen towards the pubic area. Needed a pad (mesh?).

Straightforward with no complications. I thought I would have had to lie still and wait for the natural process of recovery. NO SUCH LUXURY. Was told to get out of bed (the next morning) and walk up and down the corridor for at least ten minutes. To me, this sounded very dangerous as things might get strained and cause upset and pain. Words such as "you won't stretch anything and walking is best to recover quickly. Take your time, have a break and repeat the exercise" were the instructions from the nurse. Better do what I'm told and diligently paced the corridor twenty times before sitting down in an armchair. I could easily have nodded off but was spied upon and told "do another twenty" then it would be tea break time and a biscuit.

Eventually arriving back home, had two occasions for a nursing assistant to replenish whatever the pad was and ensure I was comfortable with a new fresh thingy. There was never an indication of soreness at all!

On another day, we had a new home visitor at the door, dressed similarly to NHS staff and carried a briefcase. My wife led her into the lounge. I was upstairs still in my pyjamas, being in recovery from the operation. The woman sat down and was about to remove papers from the bag as I ambled unsteadily down our stairs. We naturally expected her to address my predicament and mention further details about the hernia, in fact, she was a home assessment interviewer and wanted to chat about domestic appliances and cleaning products. I was about to show her my pad, totally innocent of her home questionnaire.

It might have been extremely embarrassing if I had done so, and we laugh every time about it. You couldn't invent it? There you go, it happened!

After the 1987 Storms

Owning a mid-terraced house that hadn't been decorated in years was the biggest challenge being on my own, but one I thoroughly enjoyed and put my heart and socks into "doing the place up" after a day's work. Older previous owners had a cat that did its jobbies where it felt, much to my shock and great annoyance, finding dry hard remains under time-worn faded carpets near the stairs. Messy buggers.

The first item I replaced was the open fireplace. I didn't want the bother of making a fire every time the weather became inclement, call me lazy but the ash remains from every fire might trigger wheezing, so that would go. A three-bar decorative electric fire looked more modern anyway.

The most strength-sapping repetitive chore was stripping off four layers of the most grotesque wallpaper you could imagine via hot water in a spray bottle and a trusty paint scraper and untold kilocalories of sweat from the physical effort. I worked in shorts, bare-chested and slippers until I considered I had done sufficiently, sometimes at two o'clock in the morning. Wanted to do everything quickly but ensuring it was done properly with a new colour-coordinated paint scheme to brighten up the grey dowdy interior. I was in charge, and everything was up to me.

The front of the house was priority and was given a freshen-up with four huge cans of Sandtex paint; carried out by a son of a lady friend.

It was a brighter tone and looked great. Meanwhile, had totally removed every inch of diabolical wallpaper down to plasterwork. It looked horrible.

Cementone was layered in a criss-cross fashion for texture instead of the usual bare wall. This product was advised to me by a junior staff member of Jewson's, the nearest retailer. It was cheaper and mixing techniques were slightly different. It had to be mixed with not-too-hot water. Wore a mask (for fumes). The results were amazing, even though I say it myself. However, the room retained the odour of drying cement for a long time. But it didn't really matter!

Sliding doors between lounge into living room and living room to kitchen were removed, rubbed down for repainting. Top rails and roller bearings were greased for ease of opening/closing and instantly slid without a squeaking sound as before.

Skirting was similarly buffed. Finally, white paint, pale grey for contrast and edged with a thin red line (took ages) made the room brighter, wider and a superb contrast to previous unmatchable colouring. I was impressed by the resulting effort. Old fluorescent lighting was replaced by a much smaller economical tube and extra under-cupboard electricity plugs were added; and threw out the appalling, thin, unsafe floor rugs. Discovered more little balls of cat crap.

I felt like a new person after attacking the last appointment, painting the second bedroom ceiling black. It created a spectacular aura and was ideal at the time. Double glazing was fitted throughout the property, a new colourful non-patterned carpet smartened the entire ground floor area plus the loose handrail leading upstairs was tightened; a cherry-red stair carpet looked perfect, and the loose, potentially dangerous old thing was thrown out (it stank).

Selling the house to the second interested couple, I made eight thousand five hundred pounds profit and for the very first time in my life, had money in my bank account! This gave me the best feeling I had in many years, could look after myself! Cook for myself, got a decent comfortable house. I was alive again.

Nearly forgot to mention the time taken to "modernise" my house... 3 years.

Did almost everything on my own, working into the early hours. Loved it!

Then met my beautiful future wife; via a friend of a friend that was in the same position as me, divorced, on their own, house owner, same amount of time married. With a Vauxhall Chevette that was as decorative and head-turning as she was! Clouds against the blue background were hand-painted along with grass along the bottom of the doors, a butterfly, a bright yellow sun; the driver's door couldn't be opened except from the passenger's side and other tiny insects I can't remember. I replaced a water pump, so Dawn knew I could fix cars.

It refused to start one winter's evening after a birthday party when it had to be bump-started by people attending the event. All before we got engaged!

Going back to the early nineteen-sixties, within a musical interest, I sang with a superbly fit London racing cyclist named Alan Ball and duetted Everly Brothers songs, sitting on an ascending staircase of the Airmen's Mess dining hall at Marham. The acoustics were fantastic for such songs. People must have liked it as well, because several sat or stood at the bottom of the stairs and appreciatively clapped and whistled. To this day, hearing Everly Brothers songs, I am taken back to the wide space of the stairs and inwardly sigh at singing favourite hit songs (plus an audience full of admiration towards those old tunes of yesteryear!).

Of all "musical aspects," those unrehearsed sing-songs would rate the highest and I will never forget a genuine thrill of generous applause for two complete amateurs doing something they liked. Music is a wonderful thing to bring people together. And those distant memories of drumming will equally stay within my mind and never disappear! That's for sure!

Perhaps, one day, I will revisit the current thriving, vital Norfolk RAF station and listen carefully for those echoing bygone pop tunes, sitting on the same stairs as I did so long ago, who knows? Miracles can happen.

As far as my octogenarian memory goes, there comes a time when vivid recollections tend to alter to misty memories or faint fractures of facts. Before these factors slowly engulf what remains within my "revisiting the past" genre, that eventual time is rapidly approaching its hitch-up to the horse rail or handing over keys on the final day of work, "time and tide change for no man." I still have great recall going back to those ridiculously young trainee years learning what was a mountain of working procedures, recipes, practical usage of items such as knives, cleavers, hacksaw (for cutting through bones), sharpening knives on a steel, remembering dozens of useful hints the ex-chefs related through their years of experience, the list was endless and indeed, to immature untrained youths, something unobtainable sitting at a desk copying written stuff on a blackboard.

As the monkey said when he threw a clock out of a window... TIME FLIES.

I sincerely hope the oddball contents and factual descriptions have been of interest. Nothing has been added to sensationalise text or over-elaborate a topic. EVERYTHING was part of my varied, amusing, health-issues existence, although a few instances might appear as unusual, nothing has been written to falsify facts. I have "disguised" certain graphic words for censorship reasons.

The first three cooking items we did were "baking powder goods," raspberry buns, rock cakes and sultana scones. I can smell them now!

What an achievement. We (the 35th entry) had cooked something as if it was the first event of progress, WHICH IT WAS. The sorry thing was, we only had a sample taste of what we had cooked. The remainder was taken into another kitchen to be presented to other trainees. I distinctly remember one of the long descriptions written on the blackboard to relate bread factors; "A diagrammatic representation of the composition of a loaf of bread" WowWee.

Basic tools of the trade were demonstrated with an emphasis on safety. A fad (now banned, for good reasons) was wearing a chef's belt around the waist containing a set of jobbing knives, from a small paring knife, fish-filleting (thin-blade) knife, long narrow tapering ham knife, boning knife, general-use carving knife and a must-have item, a metal steel. This was all the go until (so we were told) a French chef skidded while walking through a swinging servery door and fell upon the belt and unfortunately a knife pierced his heart and he died from blood loss. Hence the banning for future use. Butchery was certainly different. Using cleavers, hacksaws, large carving knives and boning knives, to dissect beef into steaks, stewing meat, mince, removing cod fat and kidney suet (which was rendered down into oil). Keeping bones to add to a stockpot towards making gravy and sauces. Nothing was wasted. Similar system with pork but mainly for sausages.

Deboning a side of smoked bacon was a wonderful achievement if you could manage to observe the tutor's demos. There were many portions associated with bacon, and the ham hock was first to be sorted for salads as well as gammon steaks, which were favourites for tea meals. Too popular in summer.

I regularly deboned a side of bacon on night shift, on my own. Phew!

A few soups were made obsolete during reclassification such as mulligatawny and Scotch broth. Thin consommé, thick meaty oxtail. All vegetable ingredients had to be cut into specific shapes and sizes. Potatoes had to be the same size, thickness, and length with many variations requiring precise measurements which seemed bloody silly at the time. Pont Neuf, Allumette, for example.

Sippets and croutons for soups were fiddly and time-consuming. Melba toast seemed pointless. Gravy making was the most important of basic lessons and many hints were freely given to shortcuts, which came in handy for future working in bulk cooking kitchens. There were so many things to do, remember and carry out, young minds had to adapt and quickly memorise each instruction given. Hence multi-tasking. French menus appeared. Terminologies had to be learnt. Same with recipe B's… short cuts!

Catering was not an easy trade although it was often frowned upon as a less glamorous industry. It was exceptionally physical, long hours standing on your feet, walking miles within a kitchen environment. Lifting heavy metal tins, copper-based pans, working with heavyweight mixing bowls, making pastries by the hundred. Soup by the gallon, custard too. Roasting dozens of chickens, frying hundreds of eggs for tea meals, it was and seemed to be, perpetual motion at a frenzied pace and heat from huge ovens to contend with made sweat an annoyance, while doing three things at once. You had to have a clear head, patience of a saint, ready with a smile or a joke, which assisted the shift along without hardships.

Cooking for the masses was one hell of a job, and anybody saying negative words about it should involve themselves in an early breakfast or main lunch shift. Their opinion would surely change after the experience. That I am certain of!

Next time you pay a visit to your favourite chippie, try this for a comparison. Cannot count the number of times responsible for teatime chips, which accompanied EVERYTHING served from the counters to personnel. The workload, energy required, bulk of bins containing chipped potatoes and the oil-splashed cardboard protective floor-covering danger, was the most strenuous on-the-go-all-the-while cooking tasks you could come across. It was more demanding than making fifty Scotch eggs (the very first preparation of my young trainee days) or frying three hundred eggs for tea, which is an entire box of the little yellow-eyed, spitting, splattering, stinking (flatulence) foodstuffs The chips were blanched because of the time factor. You couldn't possibly cook ad hoc and serve the quantity required each meal, so pre-cooking was necessary, and this would be done earlier, maybe by the duty cook presenting up to forty square serving tins set beside the commercial fish fryers (three or four in line) with extractor fans immediately above them. Such was the activity of the person doing the frying, the melted lard (cooking medium) would splash from the chips being removed from the fryer and drip onto the floor. Cardboard would hopefully prevent the cook from sliding on the greasy surface and soak up the liquid. It looked very messy, believe me, and I was glad no duty officer on his rounds ever popped in to see what was going on. Recently promoted young officers would do this out of bloody-mindedness, to get under the skin of the operative and ask silly, stupid questions that usually had nothing to do with the job in hand. They did that sort of thing! I talk from experience!

Although each proficient cook could do pastries, each mess (usually) had its own pastry cook. The assortment and quantity of an average mess outlet was astounding and sustained a truly mouth-watering selection of goodies. Ranging from cold sweets like fruit jellies, sorbets, instant milk-based fruit-flavoured custards, to rice pudding, baked apples, mixed fruit pies, flans, steamed lemon/chocolate/jam roly-poly puddings, bread and butter puddings... no wonder there were hardly any complaints in the front-of-mess-hall "suggestions box." Plus, if diets were insisted upon, these could be pre-ordered. Boxers, athletes and specialist swimmers were given alternative menus to select items. They were spoilt for choice, but even then, someone might offer a little moan. Smart arse!

One of our first classroom tuitions was on a subject which years later, I would become fully employed as baker and bread maker extraordinaire, in the last RAF Middle East bakery, in Tobruk, Libya, North Africa. Where, as a team of only six Brits and two Arab assistants, we mixed, shaped, cooked, sliced and packaged thousands of loaves of bread and rolls for the mixed military personnel and NAAFI staff in the garrison. These coincidences cannot be explained, but it does make you wonder how and why circumstances can bridge eras and distances? Beyond me!

When I read or am told by former personnel they served in many postings from all over the globe, I was lucky, only being sent to Norfolk, the Highlands of Scotland, Huntingdonshire, abroad for two heavenly sun-baked years in North Africa before ending my service career at Coltishall, Norfolk.

Whereas others were sent on detachments or courses all over the place, I attended short-stay detachments. One was Newhaven near Brighton, assisting with the closure of a marine craft unit. That was straightforward. Busy though.

I drove my Black Bess Ford Zephyr from Norwich to Tilbury Docks, where I was told, "We ain't had a f..king ferry here, mate, for many years, you'll hafta go back along the line." How I got to very busy traffic under a tunnel (Dartford?) I don't remember a single thing, but driving back along the Tonbridge Wells Road, ascending a gradual incline, the column-change gear lever snapped from its welded joint, and holding the stub firmly, I had to change gear all the way back to Coltishall Norfolk using the palm of my left hand. The next morning, my arm from wrist to elbow was swollen. I was given two days off. That I can recall.

Neatishead near Coltishall was a dull, uninteresting brief stay. I fail to recall why I went there. It had been a top-secret underground radar base, and the only thing I knew about it was that an airman had been decapitated in a freak accident. It is a museum nowadays. Tarrant Rushton in Dorset saw me staying in an ex-army windowless radio-transmitting vehicle and feeling agoraphobic for two days.

It was a combined RAF/Army exercise trailing aircraft from God only knows where, across the North Sea. Such a waste of time, sitting in a chair watching a green fluttering screen with flashes and blimps jumping across a wobbling line with hiccups. The guy with me was foreign, and we didn't speak at all.

The only nice thing was that the beer in the nearest little crowded smoke-filled pub was wonderfully refreshing to a dry throat that hadn't had a drink since breakfast.

I escaped one or two potential argumentative differences with my humour. Could laugh off serious things as "not being worth the trouble" by changing the tone of conversations, whatever! Witnessing a few fisticuffs between Army and Air Force bods (associated with too much to drink), such quarrels were never worth the hassle, and I kept a distance from the melee.

It might result in group aggression. THAT was, or could be, disconcerting and lead to mass hysteria. Drink was forever an easy way for a fight.

Another detachment was to Honington in Suffolk. All I remember was there were far too many cooks working together in one kitchen, literally bumping into one another; such bad organisation, I thought!

The last brief attendance was to Blandford Forum, but the vagaries of time have completely removed whatever reason there was for being there, from my memory. Something to do with the Army?

Never classed as an event due to it lasting three seconds, down at the rocks in Tobruk Harbour, where we used to dive off rocks into unbelievably clear Mediterranean water with the sun blazing down from a clear blue sky; I stood up to stretch after a swim, as the well-used, faded yellow budgie-smugglers split at both sides, and my predicament was for all to see (only five blokes) until a caring person offered me a towel. We never dried ourselves down but lounged on the abundant rocky shelf and "gonked" till we woke up! Life was extremely relaxed before a Mr Gaddafi started filling TV screens. I lived in Tobruk when King Idris reigned and saw the man himself a couple of times in his chauffeured Mercedes, surrounded by a motorcycle guard of CYDEF police/army outriders. Grand old man with a long beard!

The Queen's palace was separate from the King's, in town. On an isthmus about a mile away, armed guards could be seen close to where we dived from rocks; occasionally, they would point their rifles towards us as a warning!

Not for one moment would I have thought they might aim to kill, but by all accounts, such things were not rare. We kept to where we were safe.

There was always tall, wired fencing running along a perimeter from the old Italian buildings to the separate palace. We were aware of guards and didn't trespass past the notices forbidding entry. We did behave ourselves!

Back to the bakery. One incident that could easily have become serious was my manhandling one of the Arab assistants, who did the cleaning, helped grease the well-worn blackened bread tins and maintained the general tidiness of the interior. Abdulmullah had finished hand-priming a diesel fuel tank and locked the rear door of the room. This was immediately after I mopped the entire floor area from the proofing cabinets to Sergeant Davies's small personal office door. It took twenty minutes (on your own, without help) to-ing and fro-ing, backwards and forwards, with the heavy-headed, long-handled broom thing. I puffed out my cheeks and wiped sweat from my forehead. Then... the bloody silly sod of an Arab nonchalantly walked down the fresh-smelling, cleaned, tiled floor towards me. I went stir-crazy mad in a second. Outside, hand-cranking the pump, he stood on safety gravel mixed with tiny stones (prevention against sparks), and he hadn't wiped his flip-flop-shod feet, and left perfect impressions of his footwear all over where I had just mopped.

I grabbed hold of his thin ineffectual body and quickly, with feeling, wrapped my left arm around his neck in a wrestling half-nelson hold and called out, "Cooloo Arab zift," roughly translating, "All Arabs are s..t." Couldn't hold back my anger (which was unusual for me), gripped his neck for a second no more and let him go. I was inwardly fuming, but not exactly spitting feathers!

He slid to the floor, in fright mostly, wagging his finger at me and replying in the way that was his right, then shot out through the tall, heavy bakery entrance doors.

Ted the Bread, Sergeant Edward Davies, immediately surmised Abdulmullah would go to his nearest police station and report what had happened. "What have you done, Jon Boy?" and we got ready to end the morning shift.

The early shift was two a.m. until ten a.m., for actual mixing, proving and baking bread. Returning after teatime to slice and pack the required quota for the next day's rations. It would be cooler within the echoing building, with a sense of calm amongst the physical effort, without the loud whirring of the machines.

The sergeant was about to turn the key to lock the doors when a Land Rover of the CYDEF (Cyrenaica Defence Force... which was part police, part military) pulled up at the steps, and two armed, military-dressed Arabs quickly ran towards our departure. The senior man sitting in the front seat spoke great English and informed us that Mr Abdullaah had been attacked and assaulted and that I had sworn at the King. I was to accompany them to their depot and make a statement. We were more than surprised. Ted the Bread turned towards me and raised his eyebrows.

Before being taken away, another Land Rover halted beside the local enforcement vehicle. Two RAF snoops with holsters containing the old established Smith and Wesson stood beside me, and one said, "You won't be arrested; it's just for show really."

Which wasn't any help to the shock of going to a foreign police station. For well over an hour, I sat in an air-conditioned, almost cold room with enormous portraits of His Majesty King Idris peering down on me.

An immaculately dressed, tall, good-looking guy with the thinnest moustache I had ever seen related what had happened, according to the Arab labourer.

Everything was how it had been, nothing added, but the crux of the report pertained to what I said about the King. This I explained to another non-military man in Arab clothing, who had been writing notes. I didn't mention the King by name; it was a word spoken in anger, I insisted. Would never blaspheme any royalty; the RAF have respect for such VIPs.

That was it, and I was duly returned to the garrison by RAF staff. I had to go into town a few days later and was led through cool tall corridors, past lots of offices and rooms leading elsewhere. This time it was like an English court. A small team of bods were on my side, and a solicitor-type Egyptian spoke on my behalf. It was more serious (it felt) than my previous meeting and, I must admit, the occasion of being in a prison-like building shook me. My heart was attempting to burst through my clinging shirt.

My mouth was sandpaper dry, as I slowly eyed the entire room in a moment of panic, plus I cannot recall all that was said during the time. I was in a daze.

Don't know how long I was in the room, but my team left first. The smartly dressed man came up to where I sat and gave a smile that wouldn't have gone amiss in a toothpaste advertisement, "Your case has been admonished from offending the King. But you are to apologise and shake hands with Abdulmullah Ali Abdulmullah (the worker)," who politely said, "Thank you, Mr John, hope we are still friends?"

This incident soon found all English-speaking personnel of camp who jokingly (when my wife and family eventually came from the UK) nicknamed me THE CRIMINAL and was one more heart-stopping event to live with until St Peter gives the call to make an appointment to see Him.

A Visit to a Fair

Mother, in a moment of foresight and not her usual tight-lipped persona, took my sister and I to an open field we had not walked along, although we went to school on the opposite path.

An October late afternoon air was cold but we were wrapped up against any ominous bad weather with matching mittens and I think we wore woollen bobble hats. The street paving ended to get onto a well-trodden slippery grass way as we arrived at the open-air ex-council-run bus depositary. Next to a main road. Irony years later, I lived in a top-floor maisonette, opposite the old depot.

Lots of smells, lots of noise, shouts from excited kids and loud music suddenly enveloped us and our "breathe-in-the-air" ambling. Hordes of family members and teenage boys and girls came in sight. We had not known such activity. Sis and I held hands while Mother kept repeating, "Don't wander off without me, stay close together." This was all new to us.

A popular hit record of the day (era), and still currently played, *Reet Petite* by Jackie Wilson, was incessantly played from high-up speakers. Girls were bopping, laughing, screaming, and twirling fashionable dresses to the beat, clasping small purses and white handkerchiefs. It was special to us; we hadn't been to a fair, only heard them from miles away.

Hot dogs with onions, splattered with tomato sauce or mustard, were glimpsed; we had never had them. The distinctive aroma mixed with sugary sweet candyfloss, bright flickering flashing lights, whiffs of diesel and hot oil passing through with doughnuts being cooked in see-through cabinets, created much excitement, and eyes were everywhere looking at what was going on at stalls as we slowly passed. Goldfish in plastic bags had to be won by hooping a ring. Coconuts had to be knocked off a pedestal. Large jelly lollipops, toffee apples, huge creamy ice creams looked scrummy. Bubble gum was a new thing from America and took ages to chew. Cones of chips looked nice as well. We were in food heaven and gazed, perhaps in awe, at the new foodstuffs, colourful buntings, looking into distorted mirrors that made your face appear like a frog or a stick insect. We smiled. We hadn't done this before!

Huge pulsating ex-army generators provided the electricity for dozens of side shows. Gallopers (horses that bobbed up and down while circling) were full of smiling, happy, cheering kids while parents watched and waved as they went by. Bumper cars proved a must-have for teenage boys who were trying to impress young girls. Roundabouts with fibreglass snails, swans, and butterflies contained younger, smaller bodies laughing as they slowly went by. Pellet-firing air rifles had to knock metal ducks off a passing linkage to win a teddy bear, cheap toys, or balloons. But the lingering odour of diesel exhaust fumes made people sneeze if going too near the massive noisy throbbing machines.

Younger children massed around a crane machine and tried to lift many small items like packets of sweets, tiny dolls, plastic racing cars, furry woolly animals, yelling at frustrated failures.

Darts were carefully aimed from above to floor level, to numbers on coloured cards to get something worth having or a souvenir of the moment.

It was all atmospheric, thoroughly enjoyed by families (like us) who rarely experienced the hubbub and available food, let alone won a prize. It was magical. Short-lived but enjoyable. Mother gave in and bought us pink candyfloss on sticks. I loved it. Got a fright when a bit stuck to my nose.

Another remembrance was the horse-driven flat-platform open-deck "rag and bone man"; the bone aspect, however, was never apparent. Most household furniture, bits and pieces, cracked lino, threadbare carpets and rugs, bedsprings, and general rubbish were thrown up onto the cart. One disturbing, almost shocking thing happened when returning from a previous collection: inside a length of carpeting, a dead dog had been inserted and fell out onto the roadway. Kids yelled at the man and ran beside the cart, pointing to what had occurred.

Bones in those days were very important and went towards feeding a family. Placed on a flat metal tray with a little water, you slowly cooked the bones for at least two hours, turned the heat off and let the mixture cool. Marrow from the bones was the vital flavouring. It created the main taste. When cold and solid, there were three layers in the tray. The top was the "old" fat that could be used for roast potatoes and gave extra body. The watery jelly-like middle layer was added to vegetables or used towards a soup. The bottom layer was spread over bread to become a small yet welcoming foodstuff, to keep hunger at bay. Very primitive, but that was the way people existed. Mother would, at times, tell me to go to the nearest butcher and ask for any bones for the family dog. The butcher brought two thick heavy bones and wrapped them in greaseproof paper and faced me before I went out the door.

"Tell Bruce (grandfather) that'll cost him a pint at The Wherry." And handed over the wonderful bones. End of story!

Grandmother wrote her grocery requirements from a notepad, and I would go to the corner shop at the bottom of Commodore Road (an eatery today) and sit on a large hessian sack of potatoes or the chair if available and wait while a member of staff hand-picked her order. If they took a long time, as they were always busy, I had to wait longer; they added a banana or an orange to her list, such was the generosity of folk long ago. Sides of smoked bacon hung from dangerously looking hooks on an overhead rail. I liked the sound when the man serving used a hand-operated bacon slicer and duly sliced six rashers and added them to other things, in greaseproof paper or blue bags. I hadn't a basket; Gran forgot to give the usual carrier. The nearest handy-sized container was given to me, and I got a pat on the head with a "good boy" from the shopkeeper. Those were the days!

Across the road from Canary Cottage was once a two-storey electric bumper car ride circuit and amusement arcade. I was very young but recall the coloured cars, bent, burnt, rusted, upside down, in bits, and the roof was off the building due to a fire. It was not safe, but I ventured to climb in one of the undamaged cars and turned the loose wobbly steering wheel, as if driving at Le Mans. I had a vivid imagination, even as a frail little kid. I might have been an insignificant nobody but kept my brain and body busy with all kinds of adventurous tasks or went walking. I once walked from the Ministry of Food in Morton Road to the outcrop headland of Corton, alone and without fear. There was nothing to be afraid of. Not like current times.

It was a way of life without muggings, children being followed by strangers in cars, drunks shouting and swearing, beggars asking for money; it was an innocent existence. Nowadays, childhood seems to be mainly set forward following fashions and fads, no matter how silly or untidy they resemble. Wanting every new version of computer games as soon as they are on the market. If modern parents agree to maintain this kind of children's respectability, then they must bear the consequence of bringing up their young ones who will never realise the true value of things in life. Everything is available with a cash card, which children from ten years old onwards appear to own. It's wrong!

One of my friend's parents knew we didn't own a TV and asked me to go to their house in St. Margarets Road on Saturday evenings. I watched *Quatermass* at the time, an extremely scary science-fiction programme.

Saw *6-5 Special*, which had pop singers and bands; that was good. My ride back was easy-peezy. Looking back, it was frightening, to be honest.

Put my legs up on the crossbar and whizz down the high street until slowing down for Herring Fishery Score and the descending steep, frightening, bumpy road to Christ Church and home.

A basic vital item was to do with toilets. We rarely used "proper" toilet rolls as one uncle was a delivery driver to a wholesale fruit and vegetable company. He supplied us with empty cheese boxes for the fire, which was welcome. I removed the wire and U-pins holding the wiring. Best of all, which was comical but important, we utilised orange wrappers, thin colourful tissue paper. Carefully stretching it taut and pressing it flat was most useful and comforting. Much softer than daily newspaper, although delicate and thin.

Associated with my many allergies when younger, gradually, and it took years before any recognised results saw daylight, thank heavens. It was horrible and embarrassing during summer months, with the air full of minute flying things as well as unseen effluvia from diesel engines, car exhausts, underground sewers being cleaned, train smoke, chimney soot, and the gas works. It was not until my late thirties that I made up my mind to get something done to eliminate constant congestion. I attended a terrific acupuncture clinic in Norwich, Darquawi in Colegate, run by Muslim staff who, over a two-year span, made my life that bit more enjoyable from the many sessions endured. Acupuncture needles were, without any feeling of discomfort, added to my reclined, shirtless, and sockless body. A small black box on the floor had thin wires leading from it to my earlobes. The practitioner said, "When you feel a tickling, tell me." I was literally plugged into the mains. A sensation like cold water running over your fingers was felt.

Electricity probes hidden meridian lines that get agitated by the incoming current, thus energising each chosen point of application by invisible stimulatory pulses. Sounds complicated, but the satisfying, relaxing procedure is so calm, without pain, I fell asleep twice and was awakened when my time was up.

It is so peaceful and soothing, you cannot help falling into nodding off by the stimulus.

I lay for about half an hour before being unplugged, then another measure of torture was appointed to my white ten-and-a-half-stone body: a Moxa wand of compressed herbs, lit by a taper until the tip was red-hot and glowing. To this, burning chest hair was exposed for the first time as the green object, about an inch off my skin, was slowly moved from chest to belly button area, in a slow movement, up and down, at a controlled speed (by a practitioner). The penetrating heat was remarkable, hot as hell but remarkable. It was as though the sun pinpointed a single laser-like ray into my bones, and heat coursed through my chest, opening a space that wasn't there before. Thirty-three one-and-a-half-inch-long acupuncture needles were applied over my body, both prone and supine.

One on the crown of my balding head. In both earlobes. Between my eyes. Middle of my chest. Among fingers AND TOES, my lower thighs, and ankles.

The heat lasted roughly fifteen minutes. On completion, walking out into bright sunlight and unscented air, I felt like I was walking above street level with a distant throbbing traversing my body. That's how it felt. The noise of traffic was also louder.

I was told to lose weight. Eat more fruit, fish, rice, and lentils. No cakes or ANY dairy products. Drink lots of water or fruit juices. No chocolates. Grief!

A cliché, maybe, but I felt like a new man a few weeks after my treatment.

Most allergic symptoms were absent, and breathing improved dramatically. I also stopped eating white bread, although the bran and other brown breads were not my choice. Drank lots of prune juice. Loved figs and dates.

Stopped having fried stuff, and over the months, it seemed I could hear better; everything was without muffles or buzzing. However, tinnitus reared its ugly head many years later, which was one more thing to go through!

A drifter crew's room…

Entering a drifter's crew room, you were immediately aware of cleaning smells which teased the olfactory sensors. Every surface sparkled, especially brass fittings: portholes, overhead handrails, and pipe connections that disappeared through panels into another section of the ship. There was no electricity in older vessels; the norm was high-up suspended oil lamps. Some paraffin.

Each crew member had a ridiculously cramped bedspace. A thin curtain was pulled across to give privacy. This was from where the crew ate, chatted, smoked, and slept during each given period at sea. Their home was tossed, rocked, rolled, and creaked from water breaking against the hull in all kinds of winds, rains, and screaming gales.

A triangular wooden slatted table spread itself within the space. This lipped piece of furniture retained plates from moving from one corner of the table to the other. It must have been bloody crazy if all the crew were eating at the same time. There was little room to move and usually dined while still in the traditional sou'wester, thigh-high boots, and cold-weather gear. Father had been a cook but also assisted with hauling in the herring nets after midnight during the main fishing months. It was a physically demanding trade and one that had danger on every trip. He told me he missed going out on the Guava, which tragically was lost at sea with all hands. Had missed a train connection the day before and stayed overnight in a pub, hence missing the outgoing trip!

I was so sad he died because I wanted to ask him so many things.

When we went to see his mates, I was forever questioned, "You going to be a fisherman?" Father replied, "I don't think so." Another amusing statement was "Nearly your height, Bobby," to which he ruffled my hair and winked.

He knew lots of fishermen and would take me to pubs where I had to wait and stand outside for him. He talked about foreign lands and transport, could quote long stanzas of prose/poetry, knew speeches, and always spoke in a gentle, quiet tone, never raised his voice to me. But I never got to know him the way shore-bound children connect with fathers. He went on a fishing trip and I never saw him again. I loved my dad, Robert William Day!

Old tunes at first school, during games in the playground.

Here we go round the mulberry bush, the mulberry bush, the mulberry bush.

Here we go round the mulberry bush, on a cold and frosty morning.

This is the way we wash our hands, wash our hands, wash our hands.

This is the way we wash our hands, on a cold and frosty morning.

This is the way we clean our teeth, clean our teeth, clean our teeth.

This is the way we clean our teeth on a cold and frosty morning.

This is the way we brush our clothes, brush our clothes, brush our clothes.

This is the way we brush our clothes on a cold and frosty morning.

This is the way we shine our shoes, shine our shoes, shine our shoes.

This is the way we shine our shoes on a cold and frosty morning. (I think it had other verses)

One potato, two potato, three potato, four. Five potato, six potato, seven potato more, and O.U.T. spells out.

Friends in a circle clenched their own hands into a fist and gently hit bottom and top of hands (resembling potatoes), and the person at the letter T leaves the circle. Repeat until only one person remains.

Polly put the kettle on, Polly put the kettle on, Polly put the kettle on for you and me, Suki, take it off again, Suki, take it off again, Suki, take it off again, we'll all have tea.

Never really knew what this was about.

Additional info of grandfather's allotment.

It must have been two hundred feet in length and thirty feet wide, on an ascending incline. Had sown all the vegetables himself; fruit bushes were there when he arrived. All vegetation was in neat, measured double and triple rows, with clumps of tall rhubarb. Wildflowers, ferns, and decorative grasses grew beside a narrow well-trodden flattened grass path.

A gate divided the allotment from the garden. A compost heap bordered the neighbours' fencing and walls. Enormously tall thistles peeped out across a mass of greenery. I was introduced to an oddity in vegetables: KOHL RABI.

When both grandparents died, the entire allotment was purchased by a holiday booking company and turned into their car park. Currently, the company is for sale.

I saw him painstakingly dig for hours after tea, until it got dark.

There was a time he had geese and fed them with a wonderfully aromatic mash that consisted mainly of old bread, vegetables, and oat-like powder. He made a small fire under a black cauldron using a paraffin block and waited until the fire was glowing. Put a large container of water on the heat and waited until it was near boiling point, then added the mash, bread, and vegetables and stirred the mixture. It smelt good enough to eat!

It was left to go cold, and the geese were fed the delightful porridge facsimile.

He also created a great idea to lengthen the time the fire kept alight. Mixing cement powder with coal dust, he made briquettes to be placed (when solid brick-shaped) within the fire, which lasted for ages. The ash was strewn between various plants as an additive towards a flourishing bloom. More recycling.

He also had an addiction to geraniums, had dozens of them, all the same colour. Used to swap them for eggs.

The tunnel & wrag worms…

Two friends from school and I occasionally played near the most easterly point in Great Britain. No picturesque structure or defining indication of the fact; and nearby the gasworks produced heat and warmth for surrounding homes. Disused three-foot-tall, ten-foot-long cast-iron tunnels, parked against heaped soil, seemed an ideal hideaway and shelter from the weather, but we thought they would also be super for a den. After barricading one end against entry and nosey peeping passers-by, one of us (not me) suggested making a fire, obviously for any winter's escapades. This was perfect, we declared. But we hadn't thought things out one hundred percent. We set about arranging a small, neat fire with newspaper, thin dry kindling sticks pinched from someone's house, and lumps of coke from a nearby heap (the remains from gas production). Matches appeared, and an air of silly excitement was felt as the match was placed beneath the sticks and paper, strewth alive, instant ignition created flames, then… bloody hell… puffs of choking clouds of smoke leapt to the ceiling of our enclosed weatherproof tunnel. We hadn't given a thought towards an outlet of sorts. As one, we hastily crawled out from our inner sanctum, coughing, sneezing, and eyes watering. That idea failed, but we paid another visit when it teemed down one Saturday afternoon, walking along the north seawall. The tunnel's original use was taking effluent (posh word for toilet by-products) out into the North Sea. Close by was a "decent" fishing spot for local anglers, who considered the outlet encouraged great catches; they were welcome to it!

I only went down once to fish, and the ancient bamboo fishing rod with paternoster my grandfather gave me broke in two and is still on the seabed. Never did any more fishing from the foreshore. Guys stayed in tents overnight, no matter the weather. I was not that keen. You had to be a certain type of person to do that. Not me.

At low tide, bordering Hamilton Dock, I wanted to see why people dug things up in the muddy, sometimes smelly, salt water, equipped with spades and forks, buckets, and wearing rubber boots. There were no railings or ladders to get onto the pebble-strewn shoreline; the only alternative was to jump down off the road level, about eight feet, might have been higher, if you were crazy enough. Far too dangerous for little me.

I took the easier, well-walked route, going towards the pier head and onto the area where people were head-down digging into the sandy beach (it wasn't an actual beach because from the water to the concrete wall escarpment, it was limited by tidal factors). The mystery of the diggers was soon solved as I neared the first (of three) older men. Wrag worm (ragworm). THE speciality and expensive commodity for all fishing purposes. Nothing compared to freshly caught, wriggling, multiple-centipede-legged ragworm. They looked like science-fiction creatures. Someone once related to me they were a pound each; that was years ago! Garden worms were used, but it was not the same. Less fish was caught.

I could never work out why they wanted buckets? The rubber boots, I assumed, were needed if going further into the water. It was a deep dock. The old lifeboat used to be moored up alongside a pier, which stored fuel pumped from coasters (flat-looking near-shore ships) for sea-going craft. Years later, a new lifeboat had its own custom-built covered boathouse. And a smaller rescue inflatable was parked outside the Yacht Club buildings.

One of the world's greatest maritime record holders for the fastest crossing of the Atlantic Ocean was Richard Branston's Challenger 11, built and trialled in town. I bought a long-distance telephoto lens for the occasion and only used it for that one occasion, yet one more idiosyncratic, stupid, and costly whim. Will I ever learn? I have the souvenir programme to bear witness to the wonderful event. Not sure if the record has been broken.

We also had a very peculiar-looking, ultra-modern, ocean-going monster of a boat moored up and parked for a few days beside the Lifeboat Station to let the public view the futuristic vessel. Fuelled by a secret gas formula. The sad thing was it sunk in mysterious circumstances in some far-away ocean. I have photographs of the remarkable-looking vehicle, all shiny, very pointy, acute angles, and it was remarkably fast.

Not lately, I have to add, but youngsters thought it a great thrill and amusement to jump off the dockside walls into the yacht station berthing. That was crazy. Insane. Don't know how deep it is but it was life-threatening without doubt. So many submerged, hidden mooring ropes, steel fixings, unknown objects.

Roses are red, violets are grey, they should be purple, but never mind, eh?

Why can't ostriches fly, they don't have licences.

Send me the pillow that you dream on, so darling I can dream on it too.

Three kinds of turd: custard, mustard, and you, you big tart!

What's that Durex doing on your face? F…K nose.

A few personal wishes, hopes, and opinions loiter within my old, ever-questioning mind. On-going violence, foreign interference, and potential mass rebellion must be halted before everything gets out of hand; we (the white populace) are now a minority in our own democratic once-great kingdom, we don't want to be taken over! An ominous threat is simmering! If someone kills intentionally, their life should be taken away. Return to an eye for an eye, a tooth for a tooth. Revenge. Might deter? We'll see.

There is no deterrent nowadays for preplanned criminal acts; there should be. There is no disciplinary power in court cases. It requires updating. NOW.

When a preteen, I wanted to be an architect and build towns, with tramcars, overhead railways, all-year-round weatherproof amusement arcades. Extend Clairmont Pier for pleasure craft from Essex and London to engage regular sea trips for visitors. Repurpose the once-popular electric motorboats in Kensington Gardens. They were brill. Bring new ideas into the town. What are outsider so-called experts doing to earn their obscene wages?

Install a multitude of closed-circuit television cameras (everywhere), which should eliminate anti-social behaviour incidents, be left on 24/7. Vital. Bring back traditional donkey rides, goat carts, weighing machines.

Have life-size fibreglass animals, birds, monkeys, etc…. parading up the seafront during summer months: frogs, giraffes, butterflies…ANYTHING THAT MIGHT entertain and amuse the footfall of folk. Build multi-storey car parks for future demands of parking places; there is never sufficient parking no matter where you travel. And invent a new parking ticket paying system. Everyone doesn't own an electronic 'phone. Build large toilet facilities.

No matter the severity of each assault, sex offenders should be chemically castrated, which should act as a deterrent. Change Government legislation throughout all departments, remove out-dated rules and regulations to hopefully create new, sensible, practical, and workable systems towards a better internal personnel force, to less demanding work to ridiculous schedules that on paper look feasible.

Under stress, the human reacts in anger and will have effect on workloads. No more demands. Being comfortable while at work doesn't mean having an armchair!

The more I hear about migration, the angrier my inner self reacts in ways years ago I would have never imagined thinking about, let alone writing about it.

As a member of H.M. Forces, you are not encouraged to offer comment in any way to cause bias or discriminatory bad feeling. Muslims' mass exodus to our tiny, once-respected Britain, along with other "get-on-the-bandwagon, violence-bred, non-working, blood-thirsty, women-haters," should never be allowed to step onto our beloved UK shores and get Tesco credit cards and a place to live.

Am appalled at members of Parliament and the blatant disregard they pay to humble, loyal, respectable, hard-working, tax-paying millions that require homes of their own, a decent health service, schools, dentists, improved roads and motorways, road improvements. I could continue, but it wouldn't do any good. I am and will always be proud of being British (English). Have worked since fifteen years old, man and boy, in sickness and in health, for richer or poorer, from this day forward, paid taxes, without a police record, one speeding fine, two parking tickets, twice married, but the influx of young foreign men that haven't worked, paid taxes, without knowledge of our wonderful green and pleasant land, and cannot speak English, are given benefits, makes this usually placid, calm, polite person into someone that doesn't want our precious historic, beautiful country turned into a religiously governed, non-peaceful state of unacceptable behaviour, with daily killings by people who live in another century, without compassion, respect, or feeling of regard towards other races. They consider rape as their masculine necessity.

It would be wonderful to contemplate that one day, we may be able to exist within a peaceful environment with no potential conflict from other countries, no financial restraints, free electricity, plenty of food, fish and vegetables, full-to-overflowing reservoirs, and a new Prime Minister. These opinions are from my sincere heart. I am a Brit…millions are not! Am disgusted how foreign males regard white women as chattels, to use as they wish with no opposition. Have witnessed halal killings. Despicable.

Happy birthday to you, squashed tomatoes and stew, bread and butter in the gutter, happy birthday to you.

Cocaine is God's way of saying "you are earning too much money." (Robin Williams)

The trouble with being poor is that it takes up all your time. (Willem de Kooning)

The weak shall inherit the earth, but not the mineral rights. (John Paul Getty)

TB or not TB, that is the congestion. (Woody Allen)

"I don't need you to tell me of my age, I have a bladder to do that for me." (Stephen Fry 1992)

"Where there's a will, there are relatives." (Michael Gill)

"Laugh and the world laughs with you; snore and you sleep alone." (Anthony Burgess)

"If you obey all the rules, you miss all the fun." (Katherine Hepburn)

I asked for nails but got income tax instead. (Anon)

"A chrysanthemum by any other name would be easier to spell." (William J Johnston)

"People who work sitting down get paid more than people who work standing up." (Ogden Nash)

"In Hollywood, all marriages are happy. It's trying to live together afterwards that causes problems." (Shelley Winters)

"I've been in love with the same woman for forty-one years. If my wife finds out, she'll kill me." (Henry Youngman)

"I said to the wife, 'Guess what I heard in the pub? They reckon the milkman has made love to all the women in our road, except one.'

And she said, 'I'll bet it's that stuck-up Phyllis at number 23.'" (Max Kauffmann)

"I prefer Offenbach to Bach, often." (Thomas Beecham)

"I cannot stop, must finish my coffee — off. Then listen to the magic of Prokofiev." (Anon 2025)

"A fishing rod is a stick with a hook on at one end and a fool at the other." (Samuel Johnson)

Hollywood: A place where they shoot too many pictures and not enough actors. (Walter Winchell)

"I've found peace and quiet at long last. I hope she keeps quiet." (Anon)

Currently, the amount of wind turbines standing guard all over the countryside and out at sea are providing electricity for millions of homes.

My question is a basic one, WHY CAN'T WE HAVE FREE ELECTRICITY?

There is more than adequate power from hundreds of whirly-bloody-birds (turbines) on a twenty-four-hour never-ending cycle, as well as solar panels, to at least attempt this vital heat and light source, and supply those millions of homes we constantly hear about. This is not impossible, surely? It can be accomplished without too much planning bullshit, full of technical gobbledygook rigmarole with eye-watering facts and figures to amaze and impress Mr & Mrs Average. Let this pipedream become reality. If there is so much potential power being produced, allow the populace to be warm in winter, cool in summer months by new instrumentation, improve public relations, do something different. Excess outlet (apparently) goes to the main grid, fair enough, but a percentage of that would be welcomed and appreciated by the British Isles residents.

It is feasible and needs thorough examination; it can be done. PLEASE!

Another practical, not too difficult idea would be building more seawater salination stations, to replenish the diminishing levels in our lakes, reservoirs, and farming establishments; they deserve vast improvements to an already floundering industry. According to engineers, implementation is straightforward, and once freely flowing, there should never be any more panics of droughts.

When in Libya all those decades ago, there were dozens of unattended brick sheds along the coast. The exposed pipes were jump-off places for shallow water swimming; they were old THEN!

There were no reports of pollution, leakages, or detritus. No horrid smells. Sea water is limitless, and many reservoirs would obviously benefit.

Some advertisements that were on the go (so to speak) years gone by.

Four slices a day is the well-balanced way, bread ration.

Only the crumbliest, flakiest chocolate tastes like chocolate never tasted before.

Ahhhhh, Bisto. (Gravy)

I'm a secret lemonade drinker, R Whites, R Whites.

Fresh as the moment when the pod went pop. *Birds Eye peas.*

Go to work on an egg. *(Sorry I'm late, the egg burst?)*

A Mars a day helps you work, rest, and play.

"Do you know the piano is on my foot?" — "You hum it, son, I'll play it." *(The chimpanzees' tea advert)*

"You're never alone with a Strand." *Cigarette.*

"Let the flavour flood out." *Tetley tea.*

There's a glass and a half in every bar. *Cadbury's chocolate.*

P-p-p-p-pick up a penguin, a p-p-p-p penguin. *Chocolate bar.*

"You'll wonder where the yellow went when you brush your teeth with Pepsodent." *Toothpaste.*

"The great smell of Brute." *Henry Cooper, ex-boxer — Deodorant.*

"Cool as a mountain spring." *(Menthol product?)*

Omo adds brightness to cleaner and whiteness. *Washing powder.*

Beanz meanz Heinz. *Baked beans.*

"Put a tiger in your tank." *Petrol.*

"Have a break, have a KitKat." *Chocolate.*

"Drinka Pinta Milka Day."

"My hair keeps falling out, what shall I do?" — "Put it in a cigar box."

"Do you know the difference between conversation and making love?" — "If the answer is no… lay down, I want to talk to you."

PREFACE: Peter Robson eating fish after catching eels.

CONTENTS: Cows Ought Not to Eat Nasty Turnip Stalks.

I, OOO and I cleans a big, big carpet for less than half-a-crown.
Live action foam, deep cleans, brings up carpets like new. *(Carpet cleaner)*

Over the mountains, over the sea,
That's where my heart is longing to be,
Please let the light that shines on me,
Shine on the one I love. *(Song)*

"You've been Tangoed." *(Orange-flavoured drink)*

"It's the taste!" *(Chimpanzees' tea advert)*

"Waiter, there's a fly in my soup."

"That's OK, we don't charge for it."

"Waiter, what's this fly doing in my soup?"

"It looks like the breaststroke, madam."

"Waiter, can you help me out?"

"Certainly — where did you come in?"

Thank Crunchie it's Friday.

I can't believe it's not butter. *(Margarine advert)*

All because the lady loves Cadbury's. *(Chocolate)*

Now hands that do dishes

Can feel as soft on your face

With mild green Fairy Liquid.

Smarties — buy some for Lulu. *(Round coloured chocolate sweets)*

Guinness is good for you. *(Beer advert)*

A finger of fudge is just enough

To give your kid a treat. *(Chocolate)*

Hoarse? Go suck a Zube. *(Medicinal tablet)*

Fry's Turkish Delight.

E-by golly it looks good, tastes good,

And by golly, it does you good. *(Beer)*

For mash, get SMASH. *(Powdered potato)*

Tiddly winks, the barber went to shave his father,

Cut his throat on a bar of soap...

Tiddly winks, the barber. *(Very old saying, pre-1960s)*

Soft, strong, pops-up too —

Kleenex tissues are good for you.

Eels catching alligators, father eating raw potatoes… *(Obscure?)*

I liked the product so much I bought the company. *(Remington shaver)*

All around the house, spring clean with Flash. *(Cream polish)*

Would you give your best friend your last Rolo? *(Chocolate)*

Take a tip, take a Bristol.

Today's cigarette is a Bristol —

The real cool flavour you'll never forget,

Bristol is today's cigarette.

Weetabix beats that tiredness peak. *(Cereal breakfast)*

"To pee or not to pee, that is the prostate."

(John Day, 2025)

Growing old is not for wimps.

Aches, pains, cramps, and twinges slow you down as old age takes over.

I want to live to old, old age — for something to look forward to.

If I still have teeth, that is!

"I bet you can't eat three." *(Shredded Wheat, cereal)*

Not once did I imagine living this long —

From a debilitating lung congestion,

Wheezing like a cat,

Getting out of breath and crying myself to sleep.

Thought I was the only person suffering from asthma.

Loathed the incapacity!

There is a great temptation to continue —

Too much of one subject might become over-used and monotonous,

So I will come to a halt!

This is where I intended to stop.

Two hundred pages is fair enough for subject matter

To make sufficient impression.

Hopefully, the crazy text was not too silly

And that content didn't go over the top.

My choice of hobbies are time-consuming and intense.

I love writing, inventing oddities within literary facets,

But must concentrate on putting paintbrush to canvas,

With a second collection of finished products.

Being a "sole creator" is one more challenge conquered

Since a greener-than-grass, virgin youth all those years ago.

Have ambition — age is irrelevant!

I sincerely hope my words created a smile or two.

From *An Insignificant Nobody.*

Peace and Happiness be with you!

P.S. Currently reading *Confessions of a Bookseller* by Shaun Bythell.

Someone once told me, "You must read if you're a writer."

I replied, "I don't read — but I do buy books."

After all, I've purchased John Cooper Clarke's works —

So that makes me both a reader *and* a writer.